BY WILLIAM ERNEST HOCKING

FREEDOM
of
THE PRESS

A FRAMEWORK OF PRINCIPLE

A Report from the Commission on Freedom of the Press

THE UNIVERSITY OF CHICAGO PRESS
CHICAGO · ILLINOIS

The Commission on Freedom of the Press was created to consider the freedom, functions, and responsibilities of the major agencies of mass communication in our time: newspapers, radio, motion pictures, news-gathering media, magazines, books.

The Commission is operating under a grant of funds made by Time, Inc., and Encyclopaedia Britannica, Inc., to the University of Chicago. The University administers the funds, but neither it nor the donors have any jurisdiction over the Commission, which is a nongovernment, independent group containing no members of the press, radio, or motion picture industries.

In addition to its General Report, the Commission has sponsored and has published, or will publish, a number of special studies, of which the present volume by a Commission member is one. The other members of the Commission are not responsible for the conclusions in this or other studies beyond what is printed as a statement over their signatures.

THE UNIVERSITY OF CHICAGO PRESS, CHICAGO 37
Cambridge University Press, London, W.C. 1, England
W. J. Gage & Co., Limited, Toronto 2 B, Canada

PREFACE

THE work of the Commission on Freedom of the Press has arisen out of actual conditions and has a practical aim. Its recommendations have required a prolonged immersion in facts. They emerge in part from the shape of these facts, in part from the region of ideas —general beliefs or convictions about what is better or worse in human arrangements. These two sources are actually inseparable. Ideas apart from facts may be as true and useful as the multiplication table, but they yield no direct light on special problems. Facts without ideas —though some profess to prefer them that way—can yield no light at all, since facts do not judge themselves. If they seem to do so, some idea will be found hidden among them as a stowaway. Without some belief or other, acknowledged or implied, no rational animal can make choices, reach decisions, or offer practical judgments.

Such guiding convictions have commonly been called "principles"; and we accept the name, though at some risk of prejudicing the inquiry in advance. For among us today all generalities are at a discount. It is true that general principles have been common on American lips, inasmuch as our form of society was built consciously on theory. But, perhaps for this reason, experience has brought us to the van of mankind in our distrust of "abstractions." We have learned through much pain the weasel character of the resounding political slogan; we realize how legal maxims are liable to cover double meanings; we recall the definition of philosophy as "the systematic misuse of a terminology devised for that express purpose"; we remember the dictum of Mr. Justice Holmes that "general principles do not decide concrete cases"; we are inclined to generalize about generalities and say that you never know what a generality means until you know the purpose to which it is going to be put. After all, it is the particular context which gives the "principle" whatever sense it may have. Did not Jefferson himself use the principle that "all men are created equal" to put American colonists on a par with British rulers—which was his battle—but not Virginia slaves on a par with Virginia planters—which was not his battle?

All this gives us a healthy skepticism about any particular formulation of principle. But it gives us no illusion that we can live civilized lives without principle; for principle, stated most flatly, is simply the reason for what you do or think. It is the common handle which you can offer your neighbor for the conclusion you reach; it is the essentially social element in your judgments. It is your last answer to the always legitimate question, "Why do you act as you do or think as you do?"

Until this question has been raised, one's principles may be latent or subconscious; they operate in the mind whether or not they are put into words—sometimes, one fancies, the better for not being put into words. But the effort to formulate them gives them added effect and opens them to such criticism as they may deserve. To review them in new circumstances is likely to revise one's view of what they are. It is this which leads our Commission to believe that guiding ideas which have emerged, and have been shaped, in view of the multitude of facts and experiences reviewed during two or three years of discussion, may be helpful to our fellow-citizens and perhaps promote understanding abroad of the American idea of a free press. We believe that principles such as these are needed in this era of transition; that no modern society can move intelligently into the future without an equipment of principle nor cohere for united action without a common attachment to standards, whose definition needs to be often reviewed, but whose substance is the enduring bond of the national spirit.

During these years of discussion the members of this Commission have reached a significant agreement in point of principle. The substance of that agreement is embodied in the "Summary of Principle" appended to the general report (*A Free and Responsible Press*) and following the longer statement in this volume. For readers of the present volume, this "Summary" may be used either as a résumé, as a prospectus, or as a refuge! The fuller statement and argument here given may, on the other hand, be useful as a relief from the condensed fare of the "Summary" and should serve as an explanation. This fuller statement is a personal statement and need not carry the unanimity of the "Summary." Indeed, it has seemed valuable to preserve a few of the remaining items of diverging thought in order to lend a certain three-dimensional perspective to the strong block of agreed principle.

Hence in the document that follows we have incorporated as footnotes occasional expressions of dissent by members of the Commission, in the confidence that this illustration of press freedom would add to the interest of the reader, initiate him to some extent into the course of our debate, and at the same time reveal the wide extent of the central unity. We cannot, of course, assert that all points of dissent are thus presented in footnotes; but only all that were offered. The absence of a footnote cannot be construed as a sign of unanimous assent.

With this plan in mind it was essential that one member should take responsibility for drawing up the completer statement of principle and presenting its grounds and that the Commission should be expressly relieved of responsibility for what is said in this statement. The assent of the Commission is limited to the "Summary of Principle."

To say that the following document is not the Commission's statement is not, however, to claim its substance as my own. In our discussions, full as they were of the thousand immediate and technical interests of the press, expressions of principle were constantly in the air—proposed, beaten, surviving, or possibly reborn! Ideas grew and found their linkages. While I alone am responsible for the judgments here arrived at, the following discussion bears at every point the impress of the thought of the colleagues of this Commission[1] far

1. *I cannot refrain from testifying, as the author does, to the value of the companionship and education which this Commission has afforded. As to the present study, it appears to me to contain some of the finest formulations which have come out of the work of the Commission; and I agree with the essential conclusions, including the importance of principle and the basis of the general right to liberty. I diverge on a number of points of reasoning, though rarely to the extent of outright dissent. I would distinguish*

beyond the possibility of occasional acknowledgment. Their counsel and companionship have been one of the greatest privileges of my life.

WILLIAM ERNEST HOCKING

BROOKLYN, NEW YORK
January 28, 1947

---

the generic right to liberty (within undefined limits) from its numerous concrete embodiments, including the specific arrangements which define its forms, limits, and protections. With the latter in mind, I confess to belonging to those who do not know what a generality means until they "know the purpose to which it is going to be put." I can subscribe to Hocking's more general principles precisely because I know they are not intended to be put to certain misuses to which some of his more unqualified formulations might be open.

*We seem to be enmeshed in the basic paradox of pragmatism. We face opposite dangers. There is the danger that "principles" may be applied to cases they do not fit, or may extend into the realm of concrete arrangements, and may there become converted into too-rigid rules, acting as obstacles to needed readjustments. And there is the deeper danger that the roots of principle may be eroded away, to a sterile dust bowl of conflicting interests and compromising expediencies. Believing that the latter danger is at present greater, I should, if I were a consistent pragmatist, probably commit myself unqualifiedly to such principles as can here and now be formulated, limited as they may be. It is only as a servant of the more absolute truth for which Hocking speaks so wisely that I interpose some caveats and qualifications in the succeeding pages.—*CLARK.

TABLE OF CONTENTS

1

THE NEW PROBLEM OF PRESS FREEDOM

SOMETIME during the present decade—no one knows exactly when—the printing press in Europe will have passed its five hundredth birthday. And we have just passed (in November, 1944) the three hundredth birthday of the greatest document in its early fight for freedom, John Milton's pamphlet speech to Parliament, to which (recalling the free arguments before the Athenian court) he gave the resounding title *Areopagitica*. In these its first two hundred years, between the 1440's and 1640's, the fortunes of European printing resembled those of Rousseau's mankind, "born free, but everywhere in chains."

This fact speaks much for the disturbing power which was even then recognized in the press—apart from that power who would have cared to limit its freedom? With printing, a single private voice could be carried to a nation. With none of the warning clamor inseparable from public gatherings, this voice could speak in quiet to those influential few who could read. At once a new incentive existed to learn the art of reading; the press by its mere existence was creating a "public" and not merely for books but for pamphlets. The pamphlet is agile and repeatable; it is not limited to the permanent topics of meditation suitable for great books; it has its message

1

for the day; it may therefore be a recurrent stimulus, sent out to a wide group of readers, and conveying a crop not merely of thoughts but of impulses to action. With the advent of the pamphlet, what we call "the press" begins to show its genius and its strength as a ferment. Here is an occurrence with which history is concerned, and governments, and all the watchdogs of the soul.

Without it, modernity itself would be a different tale; for when we see modernity as an era formed by ideas, the full fact is—"formed by ideas spread far and wide by that new thing, the press." The existence of the press convinced readers that they were not alone in the stimulus and response of the page before them. Even in privacy, the press page can mean a companionship, a fraternity, a "movement." The authorities were right to take notice!

Its early uses, both in China and in Europe, were, to be sure, sufficiently inspired by piety to lull apprehension. The Buddhist classics, painfully multiplied by thousands of wooden blocks, had their perils for Chinese thought; but no outsider could guess that fact.[1] And when, in A.D. 868, Wang Chieh brought out the earliest printed book we know of—a print of the Diamond Sutra "for free general distribution in order with deep reverence to perpetuate the memory of his parents"—he was winning eternal merit on the terms of the Sutra itself.[2]

1. *Indeed, no contemporary could have guessed it. It has been reserved to Hu Shih to make an inventory of the damage, or at least of the deflection, of Chinese genius due to the advent of the "Great Witch"—probably with too little gratitude for the benefits of her spell.*

2. *Under the influence of the Buddhist idea that pious repetition is itself a merit, early editions appear to have been large. The Empress Shotoku of Japan in the year A.D. 770 ordered a*

2

Gutenberg's press at Mainz in the 1450's, like Caxton's at Westminster in the 1470's, was largely in the service of the church. Both, beside major works, printed letters of indulgence, salable if not negotiable, so that the press was serving as a sort of ecclesiastical mint. Nevertheless, in 1501 Pope Alexander VI felt obliged to issue a bull against unlicensed printing, ancestor of the *Index Expurgatorius;* and by 1535 at least one monarch in Europe had made unauthorized printing a capital offense!

The technique of control was effective enough to dampen the joy of workmanship of the early printers who had begun with enthusiasm to develop a new branch of fine art. This art lay under a blight for nearly two hundred years.

MILTON'S UNLICENSED PRESS

The hand of repression was less heavy on England and on the Low Countries than elsewhere on the Continent. Yet from the Reformation onward, each change of government in England continued the censorship set up by the Catholic party, simply transferring its exercise from church to state, and changing the definitions of dangerous doctrine. In each case, together with licentious prose and verse, it was "sedition" and "heresy" that must be scotched; in each case "sedition" and "heresy" covered different thoughts.

In 1643 the orthodoxy of Tudor kings and bishops became the heresy of a Presbyterian Parliament, which lost

---

million long-life charms to be printed and distributed among the monasteries, where some still remain. Three are in the British Museum.

no time in issuing a new order requiring an official license for all printed books, pamphlets, and papers, to stop up the flood of "false forged, scandalous, seditious, libelous, and unlicensed papers .... [being put out] to the great defamation of religion and government." It is never easy for a government seated by revolution or civil war to be tolerant toward ideas it has just overcome politically and has still to fear. Yet there were those in the new anti-episcopal regime who thought that Parliament should have done better. Young Milton was among these critics. He had helped in the struggle against the royalists; he had escaped the yoke of the bishops; the yoke is now renewed by the victors: "New Presbyter is but Old Priest writ large."

Milton was an angry man, and the words he got into type in November, 1644, came from the passion of his life: "Give me the liberty to know, to utter, and to argue freely according to conscience, above all liberties." No one was curbing John Milton's liberty—though there was grumbling about his own scandalous and unlicensed tracts on divorce. But he was concerned for more than his own immunities; it became a matter of principle for him to condemn the policy, if possible to alter it, and meantime to defy it. The *Areopagitica* was issued without the required license.

The arguments Milton used for unlicensed printing were for the most part already afloat on British air; they were chiefly appeals to experience and good sense. The history of censoring in all past time is one of ill-repute .... bigotry, spite, destruction of precious work..... Milton could find the trail of the serpent in decrees of the Areopagus itself..... It does no good, for whatever is bad in the printed page brings no harm to a good man. There is no virtue in choosing good unless one knows evil, as it is the nature of the mature mind to do. . . . . Stopping avenues of evil by way of books leaves a hundred other paths open: "like that gallant man, who thought to pound up the crows by shutting his park gate." . . . . Censorship is a repellent job; a man really competent to do it will not support its tedium ("and in a hand scarce legible") and its thanklessness. . . . . Further, censorship involves the conceit that the censor himself may be admitted to knowledge which must be kept from other men of discretion, an affront to their dignity; and a discouragement to the great labor of writing, if it may be reviewed and canceled by an inferior mind. . . . . Above all, it disparages the inherent survival power of the decent and the true when they are trusted to fight their own battle.

It is in this last point that Milton comes to the nub of principle and rises to the full grandeur of his subject. His words, often quoted, may here be brought to mind again—three hundred years have not dimmed their fire: "Though all the windes of doctrin were let loose to play upon the earth, so Truth be in the field, we do injuriously by licensing and prohibiting to misdoubt her strength. Let her and Falsehood grapple; who ever knew Truth put to the wors, in a free and open encounter. Her confuting is the best and surest suppressing."

It belongs to the realism of our subject to note that Milton himself would draw a line. He would have liberty except where "writing and speech have been utterly maleficent." He would allow bishops to argue but would recommend short patience with "superstition," which he felt no doubt of being able to identify: "Popery and open superstition, which, as it extirpates all religions and ciuill supremacies, so it self should be extirpat, provided first that all charitable and compassionate means be us'd to win and regain the weak and misled."

This reservation does nothing to impugn the sincerity of Milton's great plea: for all freedom there are abuses which pass the limit of the tolerable. Some line has to be drawn. And either we are content to leave this line-drawing to the discretion of men who by their character can show a true judgment without definitions—that is to say, to censors—or we can take the trouble to define the principle which limits the original principle of freedom. For Milton this auxiliary principle seems to be that no publication can be permitted which is hostile to religion itself or to the authority of rulers, that is, to the primary assumptions of the existing public order as of 1644.

The shape of freedom as Milton saw it was not realized in his day. The offending order was not rescinded. Licensing—and penalty for not licensing—went on until after the revolution of 1688. Then, with aid from the gentle spirit of John Locke, and much weariness of the growing irksomeness of the requirement, the Licensing Act was quietly allowed by Parliament to expire (1695). Never since that time have English books required a prior governmental permission to print. But then, as in all later time, English press liberty has had its limits; its most tangible abuses could be punished after the book had appeared. As a decision of 1784 defined the situation at that time, "the liberty of the press consists in printing without any previous license, subject to the consequences of the law" (and this is essentially what

Blackstone set forth in his *Commentaries* as the English law of his day).[3] This freedom is not secured by a written formula; it is a constitutional principle after the English fashion, receiving its definition through the practice of English courts.

No one has summed up British experience on this point —up to the time of the democratic revolutions—so well as Dr. Johnson, writing in 1779:

> If nothing may be published but what civil authority shall have previously approved, power must always be the standard of truth. [When was so conclusive an argument ever put into so few words? On the other hand:]
>
> If every dreamer of innovations may propagate his projects, there can be no settlement; if every murmurer at government may diffuse discontent, there can be no peace; and if every skeptick in theology may teach his follies, there can be no religion.
>
> The remedy against these evils is to punish the authors; for it is yet allowed that every society may punish, though not prevent, the publication of opinions which that society shall think pernicious.
>
> [However, this, the prevailing solution, Dr. Johnson finds less than perfect, for:] This punishment, though it may crush the author promotes the book [American experience confirms]; and it seems not more reasonable to leave the right of printing unrestrained because writers may afterward be censured, than it would be to sleep with doors unbolted, because by our laws we can hang a thief!

The point is well taken, and in this dilemma the wise Doctor sums up as follows:

3. *Commentaries*, IV, 151. The case cited is *Rex* v. *Dean of St. Asaph's*, 4 Doug. 73, 172.

Blackstone's definition is criticized by Chafee, Free Speech in the United States, *pp. 9–10, as allowing a government by heavy punishment to suppress quite as effectively as by censorship.*

The danger of such unbounded liberty, and the danger of bounding it, have produced a problem in the science of government which human understanding seems hitherto unable to solve.

But, even as he wrote, new efforts were astir in the world.

THE CONFIDENT ERA: AMERICAN POLICY
AND JOHN STUART MILL

The age calling itself "enlightened" flowered into revolution and produced the American and French Declarations of the Rights of Man. These its own assumptions it took as final pronouncements of truth.

But as for those earlier Primary Assumptions of community life so carefully protected by Milton's limitations on liberty—why should they not fight for their survival with any other contested propositions? If they are valid and not themselves forms of superstition, let them show their worth in free and open contest with error. The American Bill of Rights made no exceptions in their favor (or in favor of any other assumptions) in its guaranty of freedom of speech and of the press against abridgment by Congress.

This bill became part of our fundamental law on December 15, 1791, one hundred and fifty-five years ago last month—let us say a century and a half ago, also a century and a half after Milton's outburst.

There were reasons for this clean sweep of emancipation. No doubt British officials in America during the period of turmoil had treated Colonial pamphleteering with a severity which had largely disappeared from England; we were reacting against British practice during this period more than against British law. But we also had a new conception of government. Our Declaration of Independence had mentioned three fundamental rights—liberty among them—which no government could remove, because government exists to secure them. There is something about liberty, we held, which does not consult the expediencies of state. To be sure, this, its new and absolute firmness, had a theological anchorage— "endowed by their Creator." Hence atheism might conceivably sap the foundations of the new republic as of the old monarchy; it might as fitly be proscribed or punished by law, as in various of the colonies it had been. But the Declaration is not explicit about the nature of the Creator; there is room for philosophical difference and inquiry; and, besides, a doctrine of this magnitude should be able to fend for itself without benefit of political support. Let speech and the press be free from the claim of even this minimum of orthodoxy!

This was the generous spirit of a great age, of all ages in history the most encouraging, the most fecund in release of energy, the most inspiring to man's self-respect: "created equal"...."unalienable rights"...."derive their just powers from the consent of the governed"! Its faith was expressed in the Declaration; its most careful statement and defense is to be found in Mill's superb essay *On Liberty*—but with a difference from the early animus: theology and natural rights are absent from the essay, the social welfare attempts to take their place.

Mill gives several impressive reasons for not reserving from the clash of open criticism any Primary Assumptions whatever. A belief held unquestioned stagnates in the mind, becomes "one prejudice the more"—a strong point in the hygiene of conviction! To suppress heresy risks the loss of discovery; in what is startling, challenging, even outrageous, there may lie a germ of invaluable novelty. To the experimental mind—and Mill, as William James recognized, was a pragmatist before pragmatism —all axioms are dubious; their fixity is their sterility: and this holds, be it observed, for the axioms of the "rights of man" as well as the assumed fixities of morality and religion. Each society must recapture for itself, on its own terms, and by its own individual explorers, the beliefs it needs to live by. Thus, in Mill's hands, liberty as a natural right or as a gift of God disappears and becomes liberty as an item in social welfare; and this welfare is reckoned, not by any inventory of pleasures, but in terms of the social value of living truth.

But even in this, the era of the liberal spirit at its height, liberty has a shape; it is not infinite. Mill would exclude forms of liberty of expression which involve tangible harm to others. In our own statutes there are laws defining and punishing libel and slander, sedition, obscenity, false branding of foods. These limits are part of the accepted picture of liberty. As one of our Supreme Court judges has recently put the matter: "Freedom of the press is not freedom from responsibility for its exercise. That there was such legal liability was so taken for granted by the framers of the First Amendment that it was not spelled out. Responsibility for its abuse was imbedded in the law."[4]

Very likely the trimming of liberty by law against abuse was taken for granted! But there was another reason for the absence of qualification in the fundamen-

4. Mr. Justice Frankfurter in *Pennekamp* v. *State of Florida* (66 S.Ct. 1029 [1946]).

10

tal document, that of emphasis. The age of the liberal spirit toward free men was also *an age of suspicion toward government*. Leaning against the evils of monarchic rule, the devisers of the republic were on guard also against their own creation. The best government was the least government, because free men would do for themselves what a self-magnifying government would too willingly do for them, and do less well. It was not merely monarchy, but government per se, that required curbing. Hence the Bill of Rights became a defense of individual citizens against the collective will of a free people.

There is a paradox in this situation. The will of a free people cannot be against its citizens; why, then, must the citizens be protected against this their own corporate will? Are the same defenses of individual liberty needed against a democracy as were needed against kings? *The answer is yes.* The Bill of Rights was not a mere illogical holdover from prerevolutionary sentiments of archyphobia, the antipathy to rulership-as-such, near-cousin to the anarchistic ideal! It is a clear-cut recognition that the community as a whole, however organized, is distinct from the sum of its members; its thought and conscience are not identical with the thought and conscience of its individual components; its resolves are separable from theirs. It cannot merely substitute itself for their inner will-processes and fruitions without canceling their precious uniqueness and losing the vital spark of their originality. So the best of free states must still protect against itself the variant freedom of its units—for their sakes, but also for its own. Laissez faire was not merely a maxim for keeping government out of economic life;

it was a general principle or admonition for keeping government out of the whole range of spontaneous human nature.

THE WORKING OF NEAR-TOTAL FREEDOM

Some immediate results of this bold experiment were such as the more cautious friends of liberty, like Dr. Johnson, would have foretold. Freed from the fear of intrusive law, human nature might be expected to show more of the inside; the rational and decent would come out, also the mean, partisan, destructive. Some of the more impulsive follies would be filtered out during the several processes of turning the mind into print—intemperate explosions had time for a look at themselves in going through two or three sets of proof—but the more durable passions, wrath, rivalry, greed, and envy, would last through. Professor Charles Beard is authority for the remark that "most of the newspapers established in the United States after the adoption of the Constitution were partisan sheets devoted to savage attacks upon party opponents. If we are to take George Washington's own statement at face value, it was scurrilous abuse by the press which drove him into retirement at the end of his second term."[5]

But the foul manners of the nation's early press could not dim its obvious importance. Self-government and a free press are inseparable. The new liberty was less a boon to the individuals who, like seventeenth-century pamphleteers, were disburdening their emotions with

5. *St. Louis Post-Dispatch Symposium on Freedom of the Press,* *1938*, p. 13.

their minds, than a necessity of an intelligent electorate. The exuberance of the rancorous aspect of a freed discussion might be expected to subside with the steadying of the new political order, as in large measure it did.

Far more important for revealing the meaning of press freedom were certain extraordinary features of the growing nation. It was not only increasing in numbers; but, as receiving and using every impact of the industrial revolution as well as of its own expanding domain, a new sense of the immense power released by liberty stole into its blood; it was haunted by visions of national destiny. Its people were animated by a sense of comradeship in an immense task which overrode all differences of status and wealth and reduced the significance of party bickering to the level of a game. With the spread of the "public school," the reading public grew faster than the population itself. Inescapably entangled in these developments, the press was chiefly affected (i) by its own changing conceptions of its task and (ii) by the transformation of its audience.

As to its task. In proportion as the press found itself in the position of a staple of common life, it became sensitive to consumer demand. Though editors were in the nature of the case for the most part self-appointed intellectual leaders, there was a business aspect which had advantages on both sides: the press had to earn its salt. By the close of the nineteenth century, news-gathering from the ends of the earth, and news-distributing to an immense audience—with editorial garnish—had become a well-organized, majestically equipped business enterprise. The one-man dynamo of early days, the owner-editor-reporter-publisher-printer had divided his labor, with a policy control in the upper brackets. There was unequaled efficiency; never had the people of a nation been so amply supplied with daily mental bread, pre-selected, predigested, and pregraded in terms of news interest. Never had so much been put at the disposal of so many for so small a cost; for a penny, everyman's coin, and every day, the ends of the earth! The supposed taste of the consumer was a determining factor in the composing room; the composing room was a determining factor in the way the outer world impinged on the consumer's mentality. This working rapport between producer and consumer was measured in the figures for circulation. The business manager, immediately aware of changes in these figures, was likely to be the heart of the enterprise, its most highly paid official, whose influence if not authority might at times invade even the editorial sanctum.

As to the audience. The early American public had its dominant sentiment but was not strong for metaphysical argument; it looked to its press for questions of the day but seldom for questions of philosophy. While the new freedom might have released all the winds of heresy, the Primary Assumptions whether of Milton's England or of Jefferson's America were seldom attacked.[6] "Free-thinking" had its own audience; found its way into books and oddments, but little into the papers. Whether for good or ill, the susceptibilities of the newspaper purchaser

---

6. *Jefferson's firm conviction that the pulpit should keep out of politics, and that politics had nothing to do with religious controversy, worked together with the constitutional separation of church and state, toward the localizing—and to some extent to the sterilizing—of theological discussion.*

14

tempered the voice of the editor; and what in other times and places the king's censor might have done, the "gentle bribery of one's own pocket book" accomplished silently in the New World. Though there were no protected truths, no crimes of heresy and sacrilege, there was little outbreak of political or theological scandal in the press as measured by the prevailing outlook in religion and the ideology of the new state.[7]

This superficial peace might have suggested that wide toleration has some kinship to indifference. But in the case of the American public a certain languor that crept over serious public discussion was due in part to the necessary *inconclusiveness* of discussion on the new basis. If one makes it a principle to commit all principle to the melting-pot of debate, what becomes of the principles which decide debate, what way has he of emerging from an endlessly renewed clash of hypotheses? In Milton's conception of a contest between truth and error, there could be a finish, because in his mind there were criteria of evidence. But if the criteria themselves became matters of contest, there could be no conclusion. As experience showed, with the wide liberty of entrance into print, public debate could not easily be summarized; as a free-for-all, it had variety and profusion of material, but it lacked terminal facilities, and there was no one to pronounce victory or defeat.

With this inconclusiveness conspired another factor, an indisposition of the public to engage in difficult think-

7. *Scandal and sensationalism began to be conspicuous with the rise of the penny press in the 1830's; they only became more prominent in the period after the Civil War, culminating in the "yellow press" in the 1890's.*—SCHLESINGER.

15

ing. America has never had a peasantry, still less a proletariat. The principles of the nation have developed a public both self-respecting and self-assured. But with the progress of the machine age and the rising level of living it has become less and less disposed to think things out. To some extent, the democratic encouragement has had the effect of flattery; having God-given rights which have cost him nothing, the citizen is easily persuaded that his opinion is already a fragment of the voice of God—or of whatever takes God's place. As a citizen he is called on to vote; he is not told, however, that he needs think before he votes. It is sufficient that he votes and that the votes are counted. Decision is a matter of weighing; and the scales have no need to think before registering the heavier scale pan. Decision by majority replaces decision by brute force—a major step toward civilized living; but it is likely to be decision by equally brute avoirdupois.

Let us think of the effect on the America press of prolonging this tendency by exaggerating the breach in the public mind of which one sees signs here and there. On the one hand, the high debate in which editors and magazine writers engage, touching at times on the Primary Assumptions. On the other hand, the voters in multitude, worrying little over editorials and so, untouched by the high debate, casting their votes, when they do, on every ground except thought—on personal liking, self-interest, crowd impulse, party attachment, angers, hopes—reasons of the stomach and the blood. The democratic process moves on; the wheel of the ballot box, like the tick of the clock, knows nothing of these motives or neglects, reaches a resultant of forces, secures a sort of happiness of the greater number—who could ask more?—and the absentee element, thought, is not missed. Philosophies spring up to reassure us on this point; man's reason is the servant of his viscera, irrational impulse is the mainspring of man; it is more candid as well as more knowing not to rationalize one's conduct or one's vote.

On liberal principles these philosophies have full right to expand their enticement before the public, confirming the citizen's indisposition to exert his mind, even on these philosophies. Thus the liberal age on its own logic of "Everything open to attack or experiment," including its original respect for a man as a holder of God-given rights, moves toward contempt for the human nature on which it has to build. Will the edifice continue to justify the original faith? Will there arrive in this land what has never existed here, a mass mind determined on the liberty to think as it pleases, which is the direct reverse of the duty to think as the evidence requires?

We have already been accused of being "hollow in the middle," having a fine literature for a thinking few, and an incredible spate of pulp magazines for the millions: "there is no intermediate literature."[8] The Russians boast they can do better; their people, they say, read Tolstoi, Turgenev, Pushkin . . . . while ours cut down forests to provide paper for incredibly vapid stories in incredibly cheap illustrated weeklies. The claim deserves looking into. But suppose the tendency to continue, the American press would find itself confronted with a very practical dilemma. Either to hold to the task

8. Ilya Ehrenburg, as reported in *Harper's Magazine*, December, 1946, p. 563.

of reason and forego the attention of the multitude; or go with the multitude and forego the task of reason. The former road would mean economic extinction; in our vernacular, it is lacking in realism. The latter would mean moral extinction, and in the end destruction of the liberal experiment.

We are not at that point. But there are symptoms. There is an absence of mental unity in our great nation. "Public" policies are not understood by the public; statesmen, abandoning the effort to explain, commonly willing to evade, are increasingly willing to deceive the people. In time of emergency we reap the consequence: there is an absence of firm morale; if war descends, the citizen knows the headlines, the immediate occasions, but not the causes; those who do the fighting can still wonder what it is all about and come through a campaign without fully discovering. The democracy of mental participation by the people in the main lines of public action runs shallow. And with its best efforts the press is unable, at the moment, to make that participation substantial and profound.

Is it possible that there is an error of principle in the shape of freedom which has been the inspiration and hope of this matchless era of courage and generosity?

At least this can be said:

It is the glory of this age that men are free to differ. But is difference a good in itself? Or is it good because and in so far as, while giving scope to individual genius, it enriches the common fund of good and truth? There is nothing freer, in our age, than the inquiry of science. Yet no one is free to be a scientist on his own version of the multiplication table or of the methods of research.

Science is a cumulative insight at the service of the race because the free endeavors of every scientist, wherever he is, observe a common discipline of thought. Civilizations are built, not haphazard, by all cumulative insights which, like those of science, enter a pattern; civilization itself is the honor paid by free individuals to the standards which define truth and excellence. It is these standards which are assumed in every "contribution to culture"; *it is these standards which unite men,* not any head-on resolve to be unified. It is a part of the groping state of thought in our time that there are cries for unity, movements for unity, demands for world unification, with a complete ignoring of the only ground upon which a spiritual being can come into unison with any other. What is that ground? A common object of thought and regard, an object which, being different from both minds and yet common to both, can give rules to both, as, governed by the same target, the shots of two marksmen converge and may actually meet. Such objects are the standard of right thinking, the requirement of justice, the firm code of an honest beauty.[9] Without these the very talents of civilization unbuild civilization.

9. *The last hundred words of this paragraph puzzle me, as to what the content of the universal principles might be. The terms "rule" and "code" suggest the kind of specific formulations that are not universal and do not need to be. But Hocking's very open-minded treatment of the Soviet code, in the pages that follow, affords indication that he does not require uniformity in such specific matters. If international co-operation waits for that, it will wait too long. And the underlying basis of a will to co-operate may be less purely intellectual than this passage suggests.—*CLARK.

—*In the phrase "a common object of thought and regard," the word "regard" is intended to meet Clark's important point that the meeting of minds is not purely intellectual. To simplify the*

19

The greater the variety within the public and the broader the liberality of the invitations to express opinion, the firmer must be the demand for recognition of these common standards, in order that variety, instead of shattering the community or producing a formless din of discordant voices, may converge to the general enrichment and promote a true commonwealth.

Experience thus puts to our regime of total liberality this question: Is there an implied but unstated premise, an unannounced condition, under which alone this shape of liberty is the best? Agreeing that all things, including alleged first principles, must be tried and nothing reserved from debate, is there not an inescapable principle involved in the process of testing principle—somewhat as Descartes found an inescapable certainty in the process of doubt. As one who doubts must be in existence to do his doubting and therefore cannot doubt his own existence, so one who tests truth must have a standard of truth at least as firm as the truth being tested and therefore cannot be devoid of all standards. If this is the case, it must be a task of the moment to bring this governing and stabilizing factor into the open and make it part of our working idea of freedom.

Otherwise, we may be not only suspected of the folly but involved in it, of applauding the maximum divergence and confusion of thought as the highest sign of liberty, the completest absence of conviction as the

---

whole statement, men meet not by seeking "unity" but by having or finding a common object of devotion. That is why they used to insist on worshiping the same god—as still, in substance, they must, in precisely the sense that scientists can meet only by worshiping the same god of truth.—W. E. H.

freest condition of mind, and the profoundest distrust of the democratic state—our own conjoint ability—as the pinnacle of political emancipation!

At the close of the nineteenth century we had begun to realize that something is lacking in the classical outlook of liberalism. To some minds this meant, not that there could be too much freedom, but that some inner quality had to go with it to make it work. To others it meant that our type of freedom had been too suspicious of the state. At this point, European experience and thought began to bear critically upon our own.

CRITICISM FROM ABROAD: THE SOVIET CONCEPT OF PRESS FREEDOM

If there is no frame of tacitly accepted standards in a community, free discussion can beget no unity of purpose. And if unity of purpose cannot be had freely, some other source of unity must be found, since nations cannot live on division alone. The most available substitute for freely reached unity is will—the will of a dictator, of a conscious and active minority, of a "leader" claiming to represent the whole community.

Belief in the reasonableness of man and in reason itself has been at low ebb in the Europe of the late nineteenth and twentieth centuries, together with most other items of the liberal creed. Will has been in demand. The reasons for this are various.

There is a limit to the fund of sweet reasonableness at any time available to meet arising issues, and the burdens placed on this fund in nineteenth-century Europe were extreme. Immense new powers coming into human hands through science and technology fired human hopes and stirred deep impulses of change, animating at the same time strong resistance to shifts of power, so that the inner tensions of all industrial societies were sharpened. It is easier for men to find common ground over an adjustment within a stable frame than over a profound social displacement. For the arising issues, conventional reason lacked the premises, just as in the international field the graver issues of empire and of the growth and decay of states had to be classed as "nonjusticiable"; the growth of law had stopped where human trouble was deepest, and there was not enough good will to span the gap. With wars and consequent breakdowns in social order, there were failures of democratic experiment (as in Germany). Liberal thinking had made its pictures for a politer world; John Stuart Mill and Karl Marx were for a time fellow-residents of the city of London insulated from each other not alone by mutual ignorance but by the fact that each saw a different set of realities and, to describe them, used a different set of ideas. To Marx the fundamental fact of society is class conflict, not amenable to Mill's type of reason or to any other, because ideas and beliefs, he thought, are the creatures of material or economic forces. This idea, planted in Europe a hundred years ago, and spreading among minds frustrated or impatient, stood ready to explain the failures of our present century to reason its way into peace and content. If thought is itself a creature of material necessity, conferences and parliaments can be but shadow-boxing; and parleys must always fail to touch oppositions rooted in the inexorable dialectic of history.[10]

10. *May not the economic necessity of making endurable terms with rival groups, with whom one must live, afford a starting-point*

Solutions can be found only in action, in the realm of will.

Where will rather than thought dictates the course of public affairs, a press free from governmental control loses at once its *raison d'être*. For such a press is bound to reflect a diversity of ideas and purposes which, on this view, admit no rational harmonizing. The more such a press were to revel in diversity, the more it would accent the necessity of the rule of decision. Hence, in general, the newer European regimes have scouted our notion of press freedom. Some of them, however, have claimed a brand of freedom of their own and have clung to a profession of democracy. Their position, taken in full view of American practice, and cleanly rejecting it, presents a comment on the American outlook not to be ignored.

Giovanni Gentile, once a spokesman for fascism in Italy, has defended that system as "democratic."[11] By a democracy, he argued, we mean a regime in which the wishes of the people govern. But what is this thing, "the wishes of the people"? No one can find it by asking the man in the street, nor all of them; the people do not, in fact, know what they want. The Duce tells them what they want; then, he does it for them; hence the people's wish is fulfilled. In most so-called "democracies" it is

---

(though not a safe or adequate basis) for accommodating differences, even by those who regard thought as an instrument for attaining material ends? It may be that, in primitive origin, but it grows outside that limitation.—CLARK.

—*On the merits of the case, I agree with Clark. What I am here presenting is not my argument but the argument followed by the European drift I am reporting.*—W. E. H.

11. "The Philosophic Basis of Fascism," *Foreign Affairs*, January, 1928.

thwarted by the very excess of the apparatus of liberty; by interminable discussion, by the "separation of powers," by the conflict of pressure groups; *ergo*, Italy, under the Duce, is the most perfect democracy in Europe!

Not to caricature Gentile's argument by oversimplifying it: "the people do not know what they want," i.e., in affairs of state and in set terms. They have indeed a surfeit of ideas, gropings, proposals; but how shall these fuse into a policy for action? They require a uniting interpretation; and unity can come only from unity, from a single will. The leader has, first, to be an intuitive listener—in this sense he must obey the people. But he must then create the uniting thought out of the diverse materials. He can use a press, a popular press, even a critical press; but only he can tell when criticism merges into antagonism and ceases to be useful!

This Italian solution of press liberty—reaffirming the intolerableness of sedition and leaving the judgment of sedition in the sole hands of the leader—is on one side a counsel of despair. Its premise that the people do not know what they want accepts the mental gulf between the citizen and the complex business of state and also the impotence of the processes of free expression to bridge the chasm between economic classes, a symbol of the chasm between human aspirations in the mass and their fulfilment. On another side, it contains a valid political insight which, though it was put to ruinous uses, we are bound to evaluate. It was a bid to regain an overall unity of national purpose by exciting in the masses a total vision of national destiny in whose behalf a will to sacrifice could be reborn. With such a vision, internal solutions otherwise hopeless become possible. The public, called on to share intimately in the great adventure, is liberated to this extent from the bondage of its own ignorance. The press, herald and minstrel of the new crusade, becomes the servant of the popular dream: *it is their press*. The Italian dream of renewed empire was corrupt and corrupted its servants; the psychological lesson remains—for a time, aided by its press, the nation marched!

In the Soviet domain the class gulf has been measurably erased, ground out in the mill of revolution. The problem of unity remains: it exists on a far wider scale than in fascist Italy and with far more varied elements. But omitting the moving and contested periphery of the vast empire, twenty years have eased overt tensions, and the age-long habits of the Russian people, locally democratic under all past despotisms, have to an appreciable extent impressed their character on the existing order. The logic of fascism must be revised for the Russian scene. For "The people do not know what they want; the Duce must tell them," we must read: "The people know at least a part of what they want; they have firm, instinctive pressures which no government desiring *morale* at home can persistently oppose." It is this inescapable tendency to assimilation between governing will and popular instinct which Ernest Barker notes as the paradox of the triumph of "a small industrial and urban class over the general mass of a country predominantly agricultural and rural"; this paradox, he says, "was less paradoxical than it seems . . . . the strength of the single party which triumphed in 1917 was not only its social basis; it was also its national basis."[12]

12. Reflections on Government, *pp. 313–14. The political form provided by political revolution, however dogmatic and*

Of all places in the world, Russia is probably the one of which generalities are most dangerous. With this caveat, it may be risked as a broad generality that in Russia the national spirit has largely displaced the abstract internationalism of the Bolshevik revolution; and a national spirit, if it is real, has always a popular base. The Soviet system professes itself an organ of the national spirit, hence democratic in substance, though rejecting the "bourgeois" apparatus of parliamentary debate. It professes to be also a regime of press freedom. The Constitution of 1936 declares (Art. 125) freedom of speech and press, especially for workingmen and their organizations. It also mentions (Art. 126) the Communist Party as "the core of all organizations of the working people, both public and state."

The major newspapers are owned by the government or some one of its several branches; they are operated by men officially selected and approved; the press as a whole, including its radio and telegraphic agencies, is a government monopoly; it is regulated by a licensing and censoring bureau, Glavlit, under the People's Commis-

---

ideological in character, are necessarily plastic to the enduring traits of national character. The Soviet régime has proclaimed three constitutions—1918, 1923, 1936—each new one showing the effect of political accommodation. J. F. Normano's statement, indicating the continuity between the old Russia of the mir and the artel and the Russia of today, appears to be broadly justified: "It was not the Communist Party, not the Politburo, not Stalin who performed the joining of Marxian theory with the needs and traditions of Russia. The ship of state returns to its historical channel sometimes without a skipper, sometimes against the skipper's wish. To Stalin's credit, he did not try to stop this process. Russian socialism became a mass phenomenon, a national phenomenon" (The Spirit of Russian Economics, pp. 148–49).

sariat of Public Instruction. Editorial opinions appearing in the press, especially in *Pravda* and *Izvestia*, are understood at home and abroad to be expressions of the Party views, or else trial balloons which the Party wishes to send out.

Under these circumstances liberty to stray from the fundamental principles of the Party line is at a minimum. The characteristic organ of what we regard as a free press, the journal of opposition, is absent. In what sense, then, can the Soviet press be regarded, or regard itself, as free?

Recently the paper Radansky Ukrania ran an editorial entitled "Allow Us To Err." Pravda, as reported by Associated Press from Moscow, printed an answer to the effect that editors have no right to make *ideological errors*, and that "this theory of the right to err really means the right to get away from our Soviet ideology, the right to be free from criticism."[13]

An imaginary official answer, pieced together from fragments of actual answers, might run as follows:

We have freedom for the voices which, in the only way ascertainable at present, speak for our united people. We have freedom, not for every conceivable press, but for the people's press. Our press is the press of all the people; and it is all the people who, running their own press through their deputies, enjoy "freedom of the press."

Our press, of course, speaks with one voice, not with a medley of voices. This is because the great and diverse community of our republic has become a working unity, certainly not in all respects, but in respect to its great practical program, and in respect to its fundamental political philosophy, its ideology. This unity, plainly manifest in our war with Germany, has grown firm through the common effort, outlook, suffering, and aims of the nation.

We have much to do to perfect this unity; we conceive our task as one of education, as well as of raising the level of livelihood

13. *New York Herald-Tribune*, August 31, 1946.

for all. In this task it cannot be pretended that discordant voices, whether of individuals, or of special groups or classes, are helpful. Having united in a gigantic task, talk disruptive of its bases could at best be only idle and speculative, inimical to the spirit of effort; at worst, it is disloyal to the community of purpose we have constantly to guard, as well as to build. The freedom which seems to be cherished elsewhere, the freedom of all to speak or publish at once, and without regard to a national undertaking, appears to us as not only of dubious significance, since not many such voices can be widely attended to, but a symptom of the absence of any serious national purpose.

Note that it is only the ideological frame which we do not allow to be shaken by dispute. Many have supposed that in Russia all criticism and opposition are suppressed. If this were true, it would to some extent justify the assertion sometimes made that the Soviet system of press freedom is the exact opposite of what others mean by liberty. But the fact is that while Soviet *ideology* is protected, Soviet *administration* may be and is freely criticized in our press, a fact which some of your journalists have reported with surprise. We reserve the strategy from discussion; the tactics, the methods, the personnel are all fair objects for criticism. And, as many of your scientists know, scientific discussion and publication are with us almost wholly free; we say "almost" because of the type of limitation which you also have recently found advisable in the public interest.

As for the general principle of protecting the ideological frame, that is not peculiar to the Soviet system. All states establish some limit to press attack upon their primary assumptions. Even your Milton declined to admit the publishing of "superstitions" inconsistent with the bases of his Puritan England. We also exclude "superstition"—for the most part quite different from the views he would ban, but to some extent coincident.

In order that the contrast may be rightly drawn, it is not, we believe, between a press under control and a press under no control. In our view there is no such thing as a wholly uncontrolled press; the question is: Who controls it? With you, individual owners and editors exercise immediate control, while all must pay respect to the prevailing economic system. With us, control is in the hands of the people, the toilers of the cities and villages as represented by their Soviets. This is to us a genuine freedom, though limited; yours gives a nominal freedom to a few, not to the many; but even those few are not, in our judgment, truly free.

28

We are bound, on our own principles, to let the Soviet spokesman state his case thus fully and with his best foot forward. So far, we are neither indorsing nor denying; we are listening. We have now three questions to put: (I) To what extent do these professions measure with performance—are there merits in either which deserve our attention? (II) Are Soviet criticisms of the American view of a free press well taken? (III) Are there intrinsic evils of the Soviet system which outweigh its advantages?[14]

For answer to the factual side of Question I, information at our command is far from adequate. Whatever the degree of internal press freedom in Russia, the flow of information across the borders is distinctly less than free; foreign press correspondents are few in number, and, as a rule, may neither see all nor tell all they see.[15]

14. *From the standpoint of debate, this discussion includes the positive liberal and Soviet cases, the Soviet rebuttal of the liberal case, but no liberal rebuttal of the Soviet claims. For this purpose, a general expression of skepticism may be sufficient, including the question of the erasing of class lines, the genuineness of the overt "working unity," the scope of "free criticism," and the comparability of the reservations in favor of basic orthodoxy under the two systems. One may point out that the Soviet system makes possible well-nigh unlimited discrepancy between explicit rule and* de facto *performance.—*CLARK.

—Clark's list of points of skepticism helpfully summarizes, in an alternative way, the questions which the imaginary Soviet statement is due to arouse. It gives me a welcome opportunity to emphasize that our Question III, "Are there intrinsic evils in the Soviet system?" dealt with on pp. 38 and 39, opens the "liberal rebuttal" of theory with which this book is largely occupied.— W. E. H.

15. *Usually a foreign correspondent can learn what the censor has struck out from his dispatch and why he has done so.*

Occasional correspondents are given greater freedom; and Soviet firmness in selecting those men whose voices it allows to go out to the wide world is understandable from various points of view.

While, in the present state of the world, the mere fact of restriction at once arouses suspicion, it is well to remember that restriction could arise not alone from a desire to conceal the truth but as well from a resolve to protect itself from false report, or again from natural *amour propre* in a land where progress is irregular and much is unready for critical inspection.

Without opening the inevitable *tu quoque* issue, we must admit that the Soviet regime has valid grounds of complaint of incompetent, irresponsible, and at times wilfully inaccurate reporting on our part. It does not forget the Riga episode of 1919. It recalls the animus with which W. L. White described conditions in his *Report from Russia*. It notes the inflamed headlining of a recent incident at Dairen, etc.

In spite of this general haze, we can form some estimate of the Soviet claim—the chief positive aspect of its theory of press freedom—that its press is the people's self-expression through their own agencies. In the nature of the case, the claim admits no literal proof or disproof; the mind of a people can hardly be brought into court to speak for itself. The question is psychological, and the psychology is that of an amorphous public mind; such a mind achieves no definite "self" except through organization. Whether any existing organization expresses "our" thought and "our" will, or whether it imposes on the masses "its" thought and 'its" will, or to what extent it is a mixture of both of these initiatives, can only be judged by indirect evidence—the degree of response on the part of the public, its sincerity, its cordiality, its disposition to go farther than necessity or fear would demand in accepting and using the press.

On the basis of such evidence, and keeping in mind the difference between the periphery and the central Soviet domain, the Soviet press does appear to find a hearty appetite for its services.

The extraordinary growth of the press is an indication that the dominant attitude of the people toward it is not that of resentful submission to a party line. Government data relate that, while at the end of the czarist regime there were roughly nine hundred newspapers with 2,700,000 circulation, there are now roughly nine thousand newspapers of all types with upward of 40,000,000 circulation. This development has certainly been stimulated by the government; so has the art of reading. There is no comparable example of rapid advance in literacy in a vast population except the contemporary Mass Education Movement in China. It is in the nature of things that at this point the efforts of government and the eagerness of the people to read should jump together.

Another element in the growth of the press is the fact that Russia has a national program, and the press is one medium for the distribution both of directives and of reports. The nature of the Russian press cannot be understood apart from its function in both the mental and the emotional co-ordination of the innumerable participants in the national effort. The press must keep up the people's willingness to sacrifice in the common cause: the Party must have access through the press to the feelings which are the springs of public will and which are able to reanimate an enthusiasm flagging through fatigue or other causes. Affirmative measures are used to maintain rapport between the press and its readers; in many of the smaller publications there is an almost personal relation between readers and staff. In times of peace, some staffs have held regular meetings with readers, while others kept the custom of an annual readers' conference discussing questions of press policy. The impression thus given that "this is your press, we are here to help you" appears lively enough to neutralize any counterimpression to the effect that "this is the government's press; it is here to keep your minds in the Party line."

In a population thus newly admitted to a modicum of public discussion, the disposition to question and check what is given them is not robust. In respect to foreign news there is practically nothing for them to check by. *Pravda* and *Izvestia*, printed simultaneously at several centers, present a version of the outer world which is the unchallenged diet of the vast audience, for better if the diet is good, for worse if it is not. Public opinion is thus molded without opposition and without the raw material on which questioning could take hold—a situation which has its ominous as well as auspicious possibilities.

The presence of great good in a national press does not automatically exclude the possibility of great evil. On the contrary, if you want to run a line of genuinely insidious propaganda, you must make a paper which is at least nine-tenths good—a principle of wide use in all lands among editors with axes to grind. The usual antidote for such poison is variety in the press. Undoubtedly in the case of Russia there is a pedagogical excuse for monolithic press utterance: it may be suited to the present stage of development of the masses.[16] But also undoubtedly that stage has a very transitory worth, and for its own health must admit—as it is beginning to do—outside and variant versions of the world's events and also of its motives.

It is to be expected that a press under government auspices should be free from some of the burdens, the excess and fustian of a commercial enterprise, and enjoy a sobriety of temper and perhaps a dulness like that of the B.B.C. The content of the Soviet press is less a pot-pourri than ours. There is no artificial play-up of crime, scandal, amusement, advertisement. Aside from the news, the dominant concern is for education, with attention to music, art, literature. There is simplicity, directness, and an absence of the tiresome pretense that writer and reader know more than they do. For relief, the cartoon flourishes, though its judgments, as expressed in its ideological stereotypes of capitalist and cleric, are so invariant as to betray a dearth of contact with changing outer facts.

Cartoonists through their ability to create symbols for thought are powerful agents of ideology, and their occupational aversion to change of type has a certain peril. For the Soviet cartoonist,

16. *As Ernest Barker puts it: "It has been a great piece of schoolmastering, practised (as schoolmastering should not be) upon adults; but it may serve as an apprenticeship to eventual independence"* (Reflections on Government, *p. 325*). *As for outside versions, the Soviet government has for some time admitted a publication of our State Department with a circulation of some 50,000, and now accepts the inauguration of broadcasts from the State Department, in which alternative versions of events, including the Moscow Conference, do actually appear.*

capitalists need to be pretty much of a kind; and it would bother him to deal with a situation in which one American capitalist, partly in the interest of the people, starts a press campaign against control of railroads by capitalists of another group and type.

One gains a total impression that, for middle Russia, the Soviet press as organ of a national effort involving a dominant outlook does at its best measurably illustrate what a "people's press" might be; and also that, unless development of the people is to be arrested at the present level, a more adequate representation of the outer world, with its variant modes of thought, will become necessary. But, apart from any question of Russian performance, the idea of a national purpose and faith pervading the life of a people with the aid of its press is a conception we need not dismiss either as devoid of value or as necessarily inconsistent with freedom.[17]

We turn to our Question II, whether we have anything to learn from Soviet criticisms of our type of press freedom.

One of these we have already touched upon, the freedom of writers, competent and incompetent, to report irresponsibly and at times untruthfully, especially on foreign affairs. This becomes a matter of international importance when private writers are allowed to disturb friendly relations by false statements. Our freedom in this respect is said to mean "freedom of political calumny, or freedom from all responsibility for such cal-

17. Sir Victor Wellesley in Diplomacy in Fetters (1944) finds the absence of an understanding and co-operative public opinion the chief "fetter." His proposals for Great Britain, which reject both the attempt to control public opinion and letting it drift without guidance, have value for us also.

umny, which is so dangerous and detrimental to the peaceful intercourse of nations and states."[18],[19] The evil is real and present—and not exclusively American. If the Soviet people have a remedy, we should welcome it. But what would the Soviet critics propose that we do about it? Would they have us check or censor private reporting in the international field? That is not their proposal. Mr. Vishinsky as a jurist invokes the legal principle that "incitement to crime is itself a crime." On this ground he argues that "lying propaganda should be made a crime in all nations." He is referring not to all lying propaganda but to such as threatens the peace of the world.[20] It should be curbed, he suggests, not by

---

18. N. Baltiinsky, "Freedom of the Press and the Responsibility of the Press," *New Times,* December 1 and December 15, 1945.

19. *One wonders whether such calumny is more helpful when systematically practiced by governmental organs.*—CLARK.

—*The* tu quoque *issue is evident and in mind. Clark will recognize the advantage of having the matter pressed, as an issue of principle and law—therefore fully reciprocal—by Soviet spokesmen, the more so as it compels both them and us to face squarely the problem of the standard of truth in national propaganda.*—W. E. H.

20. *Not all lying propaganda can be called incitement to crime. We distinguish between lying propaganda which is near to action, and lying propaganda which is remote from action; we protect the right of speakers and writers to put out what we regard as mischievous except in case of "clear and present danger," i.e., to our own community. In that case, we feel justified not merely in punishing the speaker but in stopping him. But the type of offense we now speak of introduces a new element. There is no direct danger to the community in which the speaker or writer issues his mischievous statements or appeals. The danger is to international peace, via the resentments or fears of another country, or the hatreds of his own. And there is no antecedent danger;*

35

censorship but by punishment. But who is to decide whether any statement is or is not in this sense "lying propaganda"? The complaint would ordinarily come from outside the country harboring the offender; and the judgment ought not to be in the hands of the offender's government. The Soviet reply is that such questions should be referred to an international court.

Behind the criticism of irresponsibility lies a more general and radical criticism, to the effect that the capitalist press of America is by its nature and necessity incapable of fair statements of the underlying social and international problems of our time. This criticism, which has some support in observation, is based chiefly on a priori grounds, i.e., on the Marxian tradition of the economic determination of opinion; and, as so based, it has an interesting bearing on the proposal that lying

---

the danger is made by the statement, *as it becomes a general hue and cry. The difficulties of dealing with such a situation by any legal action are very great, but the real and reciprocal character of the problem is such as ought to engage the immediate attention of the law as well as of the press. Competitive calumny can easily build up a latent war psychology on both sides; co-operative search for remedy is itself a curative project.*

The fact that the Soviet press is under government control renders its responsibility for misrepresentation definite. From the standpoint of curative action, as proposed above, this is a technical advantage. When Pravda *misinterpreted a remark of Mr. Bevin, the British government could and did make a direct appeal to Stalin. From the misdeeds of a private American press, the Soviet government has at present no appeal at law. An action of our State Department in announcing, during the recent furor over the Dairen incident, that the Soviet officials were within their rights suggests a partial remedy. Our own government might issue a statement correcting a misrepresentation justly complained of. This leaves us judges of our own nationals' offenses.*

propaganda be made a crime. For that can hardly be a crime which the culprit was necessitated to do; or, to put it the other way around, if misrepresentation is a crime, it is not economically determined. To what extent this criticism of the American press as capitalistic-*ergo*-biased is valid we shall inquire in the course of this book.[21] Here we shall only remark that if this theory of economic determination of opinion is true, the outlook of the Soviet press is equally determined, and the hope of all rational solutions as between Soviet and American views of world problems is foreclosed; we are fated to judge things in opposite senses.

There are Soviet spokesmen who accept this conclusion. The journalist Kuzmichev denounces the notion of "objectivity" as a standard no one uses:

All dissertations on "objective and complete" information are liberal hypocrisy. The aim of information does not consist in commercializing news but in educating the great mass of workers, in organizing them under the exclusive direction of the Party for clearly defined tasks. This aim will never be attained by objective reports of events. Liberty, objectivity of the press, these are fictions. Information is the means of class struggle, not a mirror to reflect events objectively.

To put this in other language, news is not to enlighten the mind; it is to equip for action. Truth has always a pragmatic, perhaps a polemic meaning; if people are on opposite sides of a class struggle, they cannot have an identical truth, an identical news. Each must see the other as making the *lie* an instrument of education and of public policy. All relations of contract, treaty, or peaceful co-operation are poisoned at the source by an inescapable duplicity in the meaning of terms. This is

21. See pp. 143–46.

quite literally the inference from the Marxian tradition as to the nature of truth and belief.

But the position is inherently self-contradictory; it defeats itself by the impossibility of professing it to the person with whom you are at any time dealing (the name "Pravda," by the way, means "truth"!). No person who today accepted this view could seriously propose to make lying propaganda a crime, for propaganda could be nothing else than lying. Nor could any such person seriously take part in any international conference or organization, or propose to bring any problem to a test of truth and principle. Nor could he reasonably take part in the common labors of science, with its world-wide acceptance of an identical criterion of truth, independent of class and nation and of all practical issues. That the Soviet government has done all these things would seem to imply that this outlook, logically hostile to all hopes of peace, has been repudiated in action—the hopefullest omen of our time.[22]

Herewith we open our Question III: Are there intrinsic evils in the Soviet system of press freedom?

That there are hardships in the Soviet practice of press control goes without saying; that there are gains we have acknowledged. But with whatever unity may be gained, whatever social utilities achieved, one thing does not exist: the press has no "rights" on its own account. Nor has any individual in Russia the "right" of free expression, the heart and essence of our system. There is much free talk in the Soviet Union, and the individual

22. See sec. 23 below, for a proposed solution of the dilemma which the Soviet government thus faces.

Russian is a vigorous debater; but his constitutional guaranty of free speech does not cover a "right" to dissent from or inquire into the ideology of the common enterprise. As with fascism, so with the Soviet system, the individual has such liberties as the state plan allows, nothing of his own. It would be hard for Mill's logic to stand against this corporate view; but for Jefferson and the Bill of Rights there would be resistance on principle; and into the validity of this point of principle it will be one of the chief tasks of this book to inquire.[23]

The unity of voices of the Soviet press has continually to be bought by the exercise of Party power; and the question arises whether a forced unity of minds can continue to be a unity. When the measuring sticks of conformity and efficiency, pertinence to the national effort and positive promotion thereof, are pushed into general literature and the arts, they have at times threatened the marvelous creativeness of the Russian spirit. And compulsory singleness, even of the Primary Assumptions of a community, cannot be long continued without loss to the maturity of a people and to their full membership in the modern world. Membership in a varied world means, for every nation, wandering amid the unorthodox, a compulsory knowledge of good and evil, learning what one is by encounter with what one is not. "Freedom to err" even in ideology must come eventually into every modern state—by its own action and in its own way. For the only living unity is the unity constantly reborn from a normal diversity.

For us the challenges presented by the Soviet experiment are to be seen less in its practices than in the pos-

23. See especially secs. 14 and 16 below.

sibilities it suggests. Does our version of press freedom submit too readily to its own evils as necessary implications of liberty? Has the liberty of each, in our system, made mincemeat of the liberty of a united all? Seeing the necessity of diversity, is it true that a certain treasuring of diversity, as if for its own sake, has encouraged the freedom of every weed as having a right to live, so that the one thing that has no freedom is—the garden?

TODAY'S PRESS IN TODAY'S COMMUNITY

The American press which confronts these criticisms and impulses from abroad is not the press of John Milton, nor yet the press of Jefferson or of John Stuart Mill. There is a continuity; there are also sweeping changes, reaching a certain culmination in the present century. It would be hazardous to argue directly from the earlier problems and solutions to the problems and solutions of freedom in our own day.

I am not now thinking of the multiformity of the press itself—which we agree shall be understood to include all media of mass communication including radio and the film—nor of the impressive advance in the technical instruments at its command. I am thinking of the varied contents of the press of today, the extraordinary congeries of interests it serves, its enormous reach, its entanglement with the economic and cultural life of the community, with politics and education.

The man who reads and he who listens live necessarily in a world of the mind, not of the senses; the words he hears or sees must stir his imagination and make him a witness of distant events. For the man of today, it is the press that draws the frontiers of the world he lives in and determines with how much inside those frontiers he shall be contemporary. The press is no longer a separable commodity of which one can ask, "Shall I or shall I not have it?" It has become a part of our mental existence. For this reason, no function exercised by the press can be indifferent to the citizen or to his community.

Of the functions which have accrued to the press since our Bill of Rights, three may deserve a word of mention: that of publicity, that of the umpire, and that of emotional interpretation.

The function of publicity is a creature of the immense and far-flung American market in which physical and mental commodities find their demand. Older American fortunes were made by productive genius; the newer by small profits on innumerable sales. Publicity destroys a mental barrier which in the enlarged community stands between wish and the sources of fulfilment; it is an essential clearing-house, a bulletin; it uses a hundred channels, among them the press. The press becomes a peddler of publicity. It becomes the organ for every group or interest requiring publicity. It serves all business, records markets, shipping, weather, strikes, laws, forecasts, advertisements. It serves all professions; reports school openings and closings, discoveries, preferments, conventions, novelties given out by the publicity departments of learned societies, even philosophical gatherings. It serves all causes and societies; it specializes on names and photographs, so that each may see himself or his sign and that all may know who is stirring things in his own corner. It maintains a corps of critics who make

41

their own publicity by knowing what and whom to praise. An immense amount of free publicity holds the public whom the advertisers wish to reach; free publicity sustains paid publicity, and the publicity bureaus know where and when to purchase space for the product or "talent" they are paid to promote. This growing obsession has completely transformed the content of the press. It is less opinion than news; and less news than publicity. And through the injection of the payment of a price, publicity undercuts the justice of the news and the significance of editorial opinion. If there were no payment, a realistic acceptance of publicity might make the newssheet or radio program a wavy "mirror" of the times; with payment it more resembles a legislature yielding its public sense under the cross-fire of pressure groups. What is "freedom" to a press distorted by the corruptions of a conscienceless publicity racket, which begins to eat out the integrity of even our schools and colleges, as well as of the arts, through throwing the premiums of advancement to those who have learned to surround their doings with a cackle of ignorant noise?

The line between legitimate and illegitimate publicity is not easy to draw. Legitimate publicity might be described as an effort on the part of the reported to second the efforts of the reporter, protecting the reported from the errors to which the reporter is liable on account of his lack of special knowledge. This implies that the reported is already recognized by the press as a proper subject for a report and is not himself creating the notion that he must be reported. In General Eisenhower's operations, publicity was a concern. In a memorandum of March, 1945, he wrote: "Proper publicity does have an effect on our troop efficiency. .... Much of the publicity has been impersonal and generalized in character .... by interesting a few good reporters in an area where some unusual action is taking or has taken place, commanders and units could be made to live before the American public rather than to exist as mere numerical designations" (Captain Butcher, *My Three Years with Eisenhower*, pp. 770–71). On the other hand, as Captain Butcher remarks, "With an army of publicity-minded generals, the news-interest points about them, some of which would be silly .... would spread a feeling of lack of respect..... Every man likes his publicity .... but the officer who indulges in it digs his own grave" (*ibid.*, p. 250). Some men are born to publicity, some achieve publicity, and some have publicity thrust upon them in spite of their efforts to escape it; the disease of our time is that the achieving of publicity has become a substitute for merit, a preoccupation which detracts from performance, and the subject matter of a business which capitalizes this disordered vanity and ambition. The press has, at present, no ordered defense.

The function of umpire is one of the favorable incidents of competition within the field of publicity. The press is necessarily sensitive to the complaint of unfair representation; if cause X gets space, cause Y will demand an equivalent. If modern art gets an article in the Sunday magazine section, the denouncers of modern art will try for an article in a similar position. Whether the press yields will depend in part on its estimate of the weight of the group, in part on its sense of fair play. It becomes clear that this balancing function has a growing social importance, even while it involves considerable embarrassment. For while every group and interest is free, under our laws, to start its own journal and edit its own news—and many do—it becomes increasingly apparent that this is not what they want, or at least not all that they want. The farmers, organized labor, want their own press; but it is not solely, or even primarily, to their own crowd that they need to state their case. It is to the nonfarmer, nonlabor crowd. This can occur only if other papers will give them space. To be sought as an umpire organ is an informal and spontaneous honor paid to those news vehicles which are dealing most responsibly with the monstrous problem of publicity. The umpire function is due for development; it has a future; the prophetic elements of the press are seeing it. Without being omni-tolerant, it embodies in a limited way the essential notion of justice within a free press.

The function of emotional interpretation has been on the whole performed unconsciously. The press reports events; it also reports the joy and sorrow involved in events, the elation or despair, the welcome or disgust with which an event is received in the soul of partici-pants or witnesses. It has become aware that the emotion of the event is itself news; and its all-intrusive cameras try to catch the grief of the mourner, the joy of the newly-wed, the smirk of givers and receivers of honor, the horror of violent death. But these, as the subjects of factual re-cording, are not the definite emotions which now con-cern us; I refer to the emotions with which emotion is reported. The press unconsciously conveys its own atti-tude toward the sorrow and the joy, the horror and the smirk. The more the press specializes in emotion as news, the more it risks treating emotion as all in the day's work, an aspect of the infinitely repeatable human comedy, an expressive effect in which there are few genu-ine coins: an emotion is, after all, a visceral reverberation due to the stimulation of certain glands of internal secre-tion—is it not? The press as a whole must be the work of the sophisticate; how can it be anything more than the daily inoculation of a people's mind with the moral disillusion of a spirit which has by necessity seen too much of the inside of the inside?

Sensationalism is the attempt to recover by a certain violence the freshness of feeling which to a jaded spirit the simple human record has lost. It is forfeiture of the ritual meaning which belongs to all human experience. The most available emotion is the laugh, and the most external; it has become the habitual American sign of enjoyment, because it is cheapest in terms of sympathetic understanding. The moral emotions are most costly, the indignant response to injustice, pity toward misery, the expansion of one's being in presence of an element of human greatness. Readers are not prepared to spend lavishly in these costly terms; and the press, whose emotional strategy must veer toward the noncommittal, tends to avert itself from the existence of moral concern. It must deal with entertainment, with the "funnies," with a crime, catastrophe, and adventure, because these involve the common emotion of semiphysical "reaction"; they make no heavy drafts on either thought or conscience or faith.

The chief difficulty with this strategy is that it is a practice of emotional untruth. It robs the event of its genuine depth. It deprives the reader of contact with his own civilization; for civilization is the just emotional appraisal of event. The chief damage done by the distortions of a meretricious publicity is that publicity is futile unless it ensnares emotion; it is successful, financially, in proportion as it is emotionally deceptive. For better or worse, the press is today one of the major factors in determining the level of the civilization in which it operates. Freedom of the press, as we now have it, means freedom to turn that level up or down. If we define ritual as a concerted attempt at adequacy of emotional interpretation, we may say that the press, by virtue of a function it has not voluntarily assumed but is actually exercising, has a ritual responsibility toward the kind of society we Americans wish to achieve.

These three new, or new-grown, functions taken together mean that the contemporary press has, without intention, moved in heavily upon the region of "culture"; it both advertises the state of culture in the nation and acts to change it. It is so much the air we breathe that the problem of its freedom becomes as much a public concern as the problem of the freedom of metropolitan chimneys and factories to exude their output into the common air, together with the wind, rain, and sunlight, the wide products of the skies.

For its own existence as an article of commerce the press must attach itself to the cutural level of the people; as John Grierson has well put it, its *Realpolitik* requires it to remain close to the masses. But in America there are no masses, in the sense which Ortega y Gasset has described;[24] or, rather, Ortega y Gasset has omitted the Socratic element in all masses, especially active in the American scene, the element of subconscious yen toward the Valid and the Eternal. The choice is not between a *Realpolitik* which finds the people where they are and leaves them there and a severance from their speech which means extinction. They must in any case be taken "where they are"; but the choice is between taking them at their easy drift or at their Socratic reality, which is

24. *In his* Revolt of the Masses, *Ortega y Gasset has characterized the "mass man" as one who claims all satisfaction for himself, resents the notion that there is a price to be paid, rejects the conditions of excellence, and insists on his right to rule.*

an inner trouble directed toward good. Barging in upon this original and central upthrust which is the essence of man, the press is unable to ignore it and equally at a loss to deal with it. It has a principle to discover.

It may still be a principle of freedom. I have in mind two symbols of architecture, each the product of free enterprise: Lower Manhattan and Theater Broadway. The Lower City is a consensus of independent actions to a total scene which lacks neither unity nor nobility nor, with all its massive power, a sensitive beauty. Broadway is likewise a consensus of independent actions to a scene devoid of all these qualities. How can individual freedom produce in its sum such diverse results? The Lower City was built by efforts which observed an unwritten common sense of neighborhood and architectural law. Broadway was built first under the impulse of competitive amusement attraction, in which the open lure tended to be lower than the play; and then under a wholly irrelevant impulse of competitive publicity which now finishes the destruction of neighborhood, proportion, justice, and dignity. In Broadway, amusement, a possible neighbor of the fine arts, and by right itself a fine art, is compelled to accept a vast public vestibule of din, pander, and horseplay, to the wide discredit of American culture in the world. A free American press seems, at the moment, to be moving passively in the direction of Broadway. It may not be a disservice to offer it this graphic image of its drift; for with equal freedom, though not without conscious effort, another possibility is before it.

This other possibility need not be the pride of the Lower City, nor need it omit all the gaiety and enticement once present in Broadway, with its invocation of that spirit of magic to whom Socrates once addressed his prayer, "Beloved Pan, and all ye other gods that haunt this place, give me beauty in the inner man!" Behind the bedizenments of Broadway even today, fleeting perfections are begotten. The passion of Broadway—deeply buried—is to create; and that is the living passion of art: but Broadway has forgotten the secret. It identifies creation with novelty, which taken alone is the formula for chaos. Creation is the marriage of the new occasion with the eternal standard. With this in mind, the press may proceed in freedom to the building of a new City.

If I were personally to challenge one product of an uncontrolled liberty more than another, it would not be the liberty to confuse public debate, nor even the perverse liberty to breed rancor in the world by maligning an ally or spreading international falsehood; it would be the *liberty to degrade,* and especially to degrade the arts, which are man's own religion of self-elevation. I confess I am angry with the defilers of this religion, and still more angry when they bleat "freedom of the press" to cover their treasons. Whether there is, and must be under our principles of liberty, a freedom to degrade will be a part of our inquiry. But it seems fair to suggest, even now, that if we reject the aid of the state as incompetent in these matters, we would seem bound to recognize of this common good we call culture that it is at once peculiarly precious and peculiarly defenseless against wanton assault by the more brutal individual impulses which still claim freedom, and that if we fight off the state, we must see our way to some other effective community protection of that common good and to its active promotion.

These contemporary problems of a free press are relatively new. Yet they are but new aspects of the unresolved issues with wide-reaching social roots which we have already encountered. The dilemma of Dr. Johnson is visible within them—whether to set harm free in the community by refusing in the interest of liberty to check it in advance, or whether to act with firmness on our best judgment for the common good, in the faith that a pruned liberty will repay the injury of pruning by a stronger growth. And the antithesis is still there between the unfettered and undisciplined liberty which is the liberty of the weeds, and the constrained liberty which is the liberty of the garden. Neither the one nor the other promises to give us the answer we seek—a shape of liberty which instead of undermining culture builds a strong, organic, and fertile culture. The answer to these questions will hardly be found within the limit of the problem of the press alone; for the press is an epitome of the intricacy and struggle of its time. These are the problems whose solution we shall be seeking in the long, schematic, and frequently tedious analysis which lies before us.

Today, in a specific sense, communication has come of age; for today, for the first time in history, at a chosen spot on the planet, the business of the planet can be carried on *in the presence of the planet*—in its immediate hearing and before long in its view. We therefore fittingly renew the conversation about the principles of liberty. There is no reason to believe that the principles of Milton or of Mill have lost their relevance, for principles by their nature are more stable and searching than the phenomena of the times; there is also no reason to believe that they are adequate without amendment.

We shall therefore move into our discussion—and through it—with a certain wariness. We shall not hasten; we shall not avoid the obvious and commonplace—as if a treatise on anatomy should omit heart, lungs, and liver because they are well known; we shall not hesitate at times to repeat. Our object is to establish usable principles with such regard to logic, and as firmly, as the subject allows. With these warnings to the reader we set about the task.

2

FREEDOM IN A CHANGING SOCIETY

IN A growing and inventive society the uses of liberty constantly develop new problems. Self-interest is explorative; its ingenuities more than keep pace with the enlargements of general welfare through the progress of science and the arts. New tools, new trickeries; ten new tools, a hundred new trickeries. To meet such abuses, the ever present instinct of repression offers first aid; liberty is abused, reef it in by law! If there is a minimum sphere of personal freedom, if there is an incompressible area which neither corrective measures nor the demands of community welfare ought to invade, there is new need to chart it. If, on the other hand, our Bill of Rights has been too free with personal freedom, if by distributing unqualified liberties with too lavish a hand we have squandered some of our moral resources as we have our forests and oils, it is time that this also be recognized.

At this moment of history all the freedoms that make up a free society are under scrutiny. To the liberal mind, liberty has often seemed not only "the first of all political goods" but almost the whole of social wisdom. This, as we commonly understand liberty, can hardly be the case; as the building of states must precede the call for liberty within states, so, continually, the forces that maintain states must hold their own with the forces which liberalize them—the two should agree, but they are seldom identical.

Individual liberty has, in general, accepted this situation; it has willingly come to terms with the demands of security and, for the most part, with the demands of order. Today, other elements of the general welfare press on the range of individual choice; public education and health limit the freedom to be ignorant (except in spots, as in Samuel Crothers' "honorable points of ignorance") or to spread contagion (except for the common cold, and even this liberty is in danger); so the subsistence of all as a concern of all, so public decency and perhaps in time public beauty—who knows? Here it is not the liberty to be a crook that is invaded; it is the liberty to be self-inclosed, to be let alone, to say in action "the public be damned." Law touches the individual today not alone with an admonition against crimes but—if only through his tax bill—with a *demand for participation* in a general enterprise. It informs him that common actions are afoot and that he is willy-nilly one of the actors; war and forest fires are no longer the only occasions of the draft. It is a serious moment in history when the liberty to be let alone—quite as sacred as any liberty to act—is abridged by the state! Yet this thing has happened; and we have to ask today whether the maxim of laissez faire, no longer adequate for a free economy, is still adequate in other spheres of liberty, as in speech and press in their contemporary scope and power.

Originally, freedom of speech and press were liberties which chiefly concerned individuals who had opinions to utter; today their readers and hearers, the consumers of opinion, are equally concerned. For the use of press freedom affects the mental diet of entire populations, qualifies the soundness of all democratic processes of thought, and in the international field becomes a mass factor affecting issues of peace and war. To the press with its present scope and equipment attaches an unprecedented power: shall this power be left to an unregulated spontaneity, or must public welfare here also impinge on freedom? Here the problems of law, a large part of the work of this Commission,[1] touch on the background of principle from which our fundamental law itself has emerged. We have to ask by what standards existing law, including our constitutional law, can itself be judged.

The fact that freedom of speech and press are entangled with other forms of liberty, such as freedom of conscience, freedom of assembly, freedom of thought, may be an initial advantage to our inquiry. It means that we can gain light on our special problem by considering the problem of liberty in general. It would indeed be a mistake to suppose that we can solve any problem of press freedom by analogy with other forms of freedom; but it would be a fatal error to suppose that we can solve press problems in isolation.

In truth, freedom of speech and press is close to the central meaning of all liberty. Where men cannot freely convey their thoughts to one another, no other liberty is secure; the way is barred for making common cause against encroachments. Where freedom of expression is present, the germ of a free society already exists and a necessary means is at hand for every extension of

1. See Zechariah Chafee, Jr., *Government and Mass Communications* (Chicago: University of Chicago Press).

liberty. Free expression is thus unique among liberties as protector and promoter of the others. And when a regime moves toward autocracy, it is by instinct that freedom of speech and of the press become the first objects of assault. The meaning of a free press is thus inseparable from the general meaning of freedom in the modern state.

1. THE GENERAL MEANING OF FREEDOM

To be free is to have the use of one's powers of action (i) without restraint or control from outside and (ii) with whatever means or equipment the action requires.

The primary suggestion of the term "freedom" is the negative one, the absence of external interference whether to suppress or to constrain. To be free is essentially to be free *from* something—some arbitrary impediment to action, some dominating power or authority. And so long as it can be taken for granted that the unhindered person has all he needs to act with—which is usually the case—this negative meaning remains the chief element of the conception.

But since freedom is for action, and action is for an end, the positive kernel of freedom lies in the ability to achieve the end; to be free means to be free *for* some accomplishment. And this implies *command of the means* to achieve the end.[2] Unless the equipment nec-

2. *The identification of freedom with the command of means, including material means, is in peculiar need of limitation, otherwise it could be extended to wipe out the difference between a free system, in which people strive for what they get, and a paternalistic one, in which everything is furnished by collective agency. Hocking would not thus extend it (sec. 7, pp. 69–71).*

essary for effective action is at hand, unrestraint may be a mockery of freedom. Tell an unprovisioned man lost in the desert that he is free to eat, drink, bathe, read, pitch a tent . . . . : no one is hindering him! For the attainment of most of these ends he might better be in prison. Unrestraint without equipment is not liberty for any end which demands equipment.

There are liberties which by definition are negations of action, the liberty *not* to work (the original liberty of the Garden of Eden, still occasionally attractive), the liberty to be let alone, the liberty to *be* alone (a part of the liberty to be let alone, also a part of the "right of privacy"), the liberty to meditate (which is supposed not to require any books or instruments, and like the interest of the yogin or the philosopher of Aristotle's ideal to require only the abeyance of distraction). These are liberties of great importance—probably of growing importance as the world fills with noise and needs. But even they, in such a world, seem to require something like a wall to fend off the crowd; and it is said that it requires means today to be entirely idle, which was, of course, not true in the Garden.

And since every significant object of civilized living has its demands for equipment, for tools, materials, space, time—in brief, its *cost*—command of the cost is in many cases the crucial ingredient of liberty. Shall we, for ex-

---

He appears to apply it to the consumer's need for the means to information but not to the newspaper wishing to have the Associated Press News Service (sec. 27 and sec. 29) and not fully to the situation of the person who has something to say but no press with which to say it, though it seems logically to apply to the latter equally (cf. sec. 10, last paragraphs, also chap. 1, n. 1). —CLARK.

—To say that equipment is a necessary factor of freedom is not to identify freedom with that factor. I point out, on the page which follows, that command of means without self-direction is not freedom. The cases raised by Clark are central to our work; one of them is dealt with on pp. 131–32. —W. E. H.

ample, say that freedom to print (allied to freedom of the press but not identical with it) exists for a man who has no press or means to get one? Unemployment is a literal unrestraint, a marked freedom from the coercions of daily toil; but as destructive of means it is the opposite of freedom *for*. In pre-war Europe, popular acceptance of totalitarian regimes was motivated by no love of tyranny but largely by insecurity of work and bread coupled with the delusive hope of gaining these ingredients of freedom by bartering away its negative element, unfettered action.

To contemporary consciousness it has become an axiom that there can be *no freedom without provision;* for a large part of mankind the main task of freedom is at the economic level; and business, as Beardsley Ruml has shown, has to share this task with politics. But it remains true that provision, work, and leisure are not enough; the most abundant provision is not human freedom unless a man remains the unhampered director of his powers of thought and action. Concrete freedom requires both factors.

2. THE VALUE OF FREEDOM

To the individual the value of his freedom lies simply in the enjoyment of his capacity for self-direction. It is not separable from the value of being alive; for to live is to act, and action *means* free action—the adjective adds nothing to the natural fact. It is only as spontaneous action is interfered with that the notion of freedom comes to consciousness or receives a name. This is why freedom arising consciously in a rejection of restraint as something intrusive and abnormal has its dominantly negative meaning.

Human life, however, does not begin in freedom. John Locke, who first committed himself to the thesis that men are born free, explained his meaning by saying that "man is born free as he is born rational." The mental maturity which makes it possible for family and society to permit the ex-minor to manage himself implies, first, that he has mind enough to choose his own ends and the means to them, and then also that he has come to use a specific sort of "reason"—the reason which patterns his own behavior so that it can go along with the similarly patterned behavior of others with a minimum of clash. He is allowed to be free when and only when he can freely shape—and that means limit—his own freedom. It is because human beings are *not* born free that they live under the increasing ambition to become so; freedom acquires an intense psychological contrast value. What the growing person comes to appreciate is that, as he is more or less free, he is more or less human.

Seeing this, he finds freedom a necessity of his being like the necessity for breathing; deprivation of liberty is a sort of suffocation. The urgency of this need is not so much expressed as satirized when we call it a "value" as if it were to be weighed and measured with other goods. Beardsley Ruml gives the true picture when he says that "the individual human animal will fight for his freedom as he would fight for his life; indeed, it is his life for which he fights."[3] Their material provision gives men their existence as creatures; their freedom marks their existence as men.

3. Beardsley Ruml, *Tomorrow's Business* (New York: Farrar & Rinehart, 1946), p. 8.

3. THE SOCIAL VALUE OF INDIVIDUAL FREEDOM

Society has an interest of its own in the freedom of its members. It is not an unalloyed interest, for individual freedom is the original hazard to social order, harmony, and united action. Screened in the case of the young by family controls, freedom is meted out by society to its new members in prudently graded instalments. The fighting interest individuals take in their freedom is due in part to the chronic incredulity with which the guardians of social stability always confront the pretense of the maturing generation to be able to manage its own course of life.

This incredulity is universal because it is universally well founded. The untried are, in fact, *not* ready for self-management and never can be; for no one can be fit for self-management without the practice of self-management. Hence the grant of freedom moves at a risk; and every first grant of freedom is premature. Nevertheless, not to grant it involves a greater risk; for to society also, as well as to its individual members, their freedom has a positive value of an imperative sort.

This value lies chiefly in the fact that society has no other mental resources than those of its members. An unfree membership is one which, just to the extent of its unfreedom, does not habitually control its actions by its own thinking and is therefore kept immature. Whatever the gains in social order and uniformity, no society can have an eventual interest in maintaining an immature membership; there can be no developed society of undeveloped individuals. Here lies the basis of democracy in human nature, which Aristotle expressed in the maxim that "the best rule is rule over the best"; an intelligent government will attempt to elicit in the greatest number that capacity for responsible thinking which is available for guiding social action. The free society, which Reinhold Niebuhr well describes as "the social dimension of the free man," is the valid society because it, and it alone, is the social dimension of full-grown men.

4. FREEDOM AS A RIGHT

In a free society specific liberties are given legal status as "rights"; procedures are set up for preventing or correcting their infringement. In the case of the fundamental freedoms, this legalization occurs because, prior to and independent of the legal recognition, such freedoms are human or moral rights which the political order ought to recognize.[4]

4. OBJECTION. *The word "rights" is used too loosely; it ought to be reserved for those claims and privileges which are recognized and protected by law. Many so-called "rights" are simply more or less reasonable wishes (like the alleged "right to happiness") presented in the form of claims upon the world in general. The "right to a job" is far more tangible and reasonable a claim, yet, unless there is some specific way in law whereby some agency is made responsible for furnishing the job, it remains an aspiration rather than a right. It would avoid confusion to refer to such aspirations as interests or wishes and not as rights.—*ANON.

—*We must by all means distinguish between interests and rights. We have been particularly careful to do this in distinguishing between the value of liberty and the right of liberty. But we have also to distinguish between legal rights and moral rights. To identify rights with legally recognized rights is to render one's self helpless before the authoritarian state; your rights, on this theory, are precisely those which the state provides you and no more. To say that you have rights which the state ought to*

The right of freedom is based on the value of freedom but is not identical with that value. It is true that, when one claims a right, he is commonly claiming something he values; but the claim of a right has a different import from the claim of a personal interest. A moral right is a value which I am not morally free to relinquish, as I am free to relinquish a personal interest. What I claim as a

_____

recognize is from this point of view a plain misuse of language. However, from the point of view of the Declaration of Independence to recognize the existence of rights prior to and independent of political enactment is the beginning of political wisdom; if governments are established "to secure these rights," the pre-existence of these rights is the whole basis of the political theory. On this issue we are with the Declaration.

The same is true of our fundamental law; the Bill of Rights assumes throughout that it is not creating rights but protecting them. Its language refers repeatedly to some "right of the people" which is not to be "abridged" or "infringed" or "impugned" by law. It thus implies their pre-existence as moral or customary rights.

In seeking a prior basis for the conception of "right" as something to which legal enactment should conform, we do not commit ourselves to any of the traditional theories of right, such as the "natural rights" theory. We are reviewing the problem.

The "natural rights" theory, however, was not entirely mistaken. Its difficulties were chiefly two: the ambiguity of the word "natural" and the plurality of the word "rights." No theory and no society can operate with a plurality of absolutes. There is one right which, as inseparable from human nature, might fairly be called natural—the right to become what one is capable of, or to do one's human task. All other rights are derivable from this one and subordinate to it.—W. E. H.

I agree that the generic rights, such as a right to some kind and degree of liberty not too far beyond what a people is ready for, exist independently of legal recognition and specifications. This principle needs to be safeguarded against the claim on behalf of current legal rulings that they have discovered and enacted specific definitions of rights and procedures for remedies which are eternally natural in the constitution of the world.—CLARK.

right, I claim for others as well as myself; in the act of asserting my own right, I obligate myself to observe theirs, including that of the person from whom I make the claim. If I yield my right, I weaken theirs.[5] Why is one not free to abandon his freedom; why may he not sell himself into slavery? Because, quite apart from his inclination, he has a duty to live as a man and assume the burden of self-guidance. He owes this to his own dignity; he owes it also to the common concern that human dignity shall be upheld. The word "right" is the announcement of an element of mutual duty in the claim of value; the addressee is bound to listen as he need not listen if I simply assert my wishes.

5. OBJECTION. *How can you say that one is not morally free to relinquish a right? A man who has the right to a trial by jury is not bound to insist on that mode of trial. He may waive his right. And if he does so, he does not necessarily let others down who may still wish to claim that right, nor prejudice his own right in a future case.*—ANON.

—*It is one thing to waive the momentary exercise of a right; quite another thing to relinquish the right itself. A man who has the right of free speech is not necessarily under obligation to talk all the time; to lapse into silence is not to abandon the right. One who has the legal right of trial by jury may waive its exercise in a specific case without renouncing his claim. Debts to me which I have a legal right to collect, I ought in general to collect, though if I refrain from doing so in specific cases for personal reasons I am still not relinquishing the right itself; if through negligence I fail to collect for a sufficiently long time, a statute of limitations may remind me that I have failed in a duty and have lost my right in that particular case.*—W. E. H.

The Lord's Prayer (Low Church version) suggests that it is not a duty to collect our debts.—HUTCHINS.

—*I retain a lingering doubt whether the "forgiveness of debts" was intended to expunge the institution of commercial credit.*—W. E. H.

5. CLAIMS OF RIGHT AS ADDRESSED TO THE STATE

Claims of right are naturally addressed to agents capable of infringing the right but also capable of understanding and observing it. They are not addressed to infants, or to animals or to impersonal agents, whatever their capacities for harm. The ground of the appeal is simply the justice of the right.[6] There is usually also a reciprocal interest of the addressee in maintaining the right; he might be in the same boat. And there is always a more general interest on his part in maintaining a social order in which rights are respected. Quite apart from any possible social punishment for disregarding the right, any one or any mixture of these considerations would incline him to listen.

Ordinarily the addressee is one's fellow-man; but certain claims of right are addressed also to society and to government which, as the agency chiefly capable of protecting them, is also chiefly capable of infringing them for real or supposed interests of its own. The various rights which we refer to collectively as the right of liberty are addressed with peculiar emphasis to the state.

For what we mean by a free society is chiefly one in which government expressly limits its own potential scope of action in respect to those freedoms which belong to the normal development of men. Here belong free thought, free conscience, free worship, free speech, freedom of the person, free assembly. Freedom of the press takes its place with these. And all of them, together

6. *A phrase which we can briefly define for our purpose as meaning that it belongs to the logic of a civilized society to be able to count, without either argument or fighting, on the enjoyment of the right in question.*

with some stipulation about property, constitute the burden of our bills of rights.

It is because of the element of duty that the claim of a basic human right may thus be addressed to the state. In modern times the state has commonly admitted a duty of its own where the conscience of the citizen is involved. But the conscience of the individual indicates his obligation to *something beyond the state,* such, for example, as the obligation of a scientist to his truth. How can the sovereign state admit what amounts to an exterior, independent, and possibly superior source of obligation on the part of its subjects?

The essential answer is that no society can have a long-time interest in developing a membership devoid of conscience, even less so than in developing a membership immature or lacking in intelligence.[7] A citizenry in so far as it is deficient in conscience is feeble in loyalty and low in morale.[8] There are auxiliary answers.

7. See above, p. 58.

8. *The regimented loyalty of totalitarian states rests on the conscience of the people, but on a form of it which is the antithesis of conscience as defined above (obligation to something beyond the state, of Socrates to his oracle, etc.). It also rests on repression of remaining dissent. Yet this loyalty seems neither feeble nor low in morale. I agree that this is an unsatisfactory basis of loyalty for any people capable of even a modest degree of freedom, and possibly in the long run an unstable basis for any people. On the dangers it involves, light is shed by an article, "Close-up of the 'Mysterious Russian,'"* New York Times Magazine Section, *November 17, 1946.*—CLARK.

—*It is true that the totalitarian state tries to persuade its people to think that the will of the state is, or ought to be, their highest law. In practice, the totalitarian state, like other states, depends for its going on a degree of spontaneous acceptance by the people of its policy. It can neither make the masses believe that two and*

Political realism counsels the recognition of such rights, inasmuch as conscience has at times shown itself to be one of the hard facts which political wishes cannot obliterate, as Bismarck learned in his *Kulturkampf*.

Further, government, having the character of will, is not necessarily devoid of conscience on its own part. The notion of sovereignty has not in modern times been regarded as inconsistent with the acceptance of moral obligation. On the contrary—as the necessities of international order compel us to recognize—the acceptance of moral obligation by the sovereign state has now become a condition of the survival of the notion of national sovereignty. If, then, the sovereign entertains his own conception of duty, whether or not embodied in a constitutional formula, it will be an integral part of that duty to respect the conscience of his citizens.

And the duty of the citizens would normally unite them with the will of the sovereign rather than separate them from it, though the risk of a conflict in their conceptions of duty remains implicit in the situation.

---

two are five nor that everything the state commands is right solely because the state commands it. Evidence for this assertion is the fact that the totalitarian state so carefully controls its press. It does so because, since it cannot obliterate the rudiments of natural conscience in the public, it must, when its ends or means are shady, manipulate the data on which that conscience acts. It cannot even carry the public along without the aid of instinctive popular resentment of wrong as a prop to its cause; it needs heroes and villains to make its business go with the necessary verve. It must therefore see to it that its people have the right heroes and the right villains. The more conscience there is, the more passion can be worked up over a skilfully distorted political picture. Conversely, if conscience could be wholly amputated, the emotional cohesion of even the totalitarian state would be lost.—W. E. H.

A Bill of Rights represents the state's acceptance of the risk involved in this ulterior allegiance of the citizen. It is a legal limitation of the sovereign by the sovereign,[9] in view of a nonpolitical duty of the individual.[10] This duty may transcend present social values and may con-

---

9. OBJECTION. *I object to this mystifying and absurd phrase and to the term "sovereign" itself. This term is ambiguous and useless; nobody can locate sovereignty in our form of government. Why not say that the Bill of Rights is a limitation of government by the people?*—ANON.

The people are sovereign, not the state. The limitation is a limitation on the state by the sovereign people.—HUTCHINS.

—Getting rid of "sovereigns" (Old Style) is easier than getting rid of the idea of supreme political power which the word has come to signify. Whether we can locate the fact or not, the question, "Who's the boss?" will always remain.

The offending phrase "limitation of the sovereign by the sovereign" seems a convenient way of indicating the important fact of self-limitation. As long as any power is limited by an outside agency, that power is neither sovereign nor free. From this the false conclusion has been drawn that sovereign power must be unlimited. Every mature individual curbs himself and remains free; the same may be true of a mature people and a mature state. If the sovereign people limit their own state or government, do they not limit themselves in their political action, saying in effect, "There is nothing which in our united power we cannot do, but there are several things we deliberately decide we will not do, so help us the Constitution"? Limitation of the boss by the boss— shall we put it that way?—W. E. H.

10. *In deferring its other interests to the individual's conscience, the state has to limit the extent to which it will or can defer its obligations. As we shall point out below (sec. 8), if an individual felt himself morally bound to a course of action endangering the state or the public order, the state might continue to respect the citizen's sense of duty but would be compelled to act upon its own line of duty, accepting the clash of judgment regarding duty. For the state is something more than a will to exist; it has also—so it must assume—a duty to exist.*

flict with specific demands of the state; but it cannot be contrary to the eventual social or political interest.

In acknowledging the individual's right to freedom (in the form of various specific liberties), there are two things which the state does not guarantee—complete freedom and unconditional freedom. Not complete freedom, for there is no such thing. Not unconditional freedom, for if freedom is made a legal right because of conscience, then if conscience were rejected by the individual, he would implicitly reject the reason for the grant of right. We shall enlarge on these two points.

6. THERE IS NO COMPLETE OR ABSOLUTE FREEDOM

It will be generally agreed that there can be no perfect unrestraint; this is usually considered to be an accident of human imperfection, or an obvious compromise necessitated by the social medium in which free action takes place—"freedom limited by the equal freedom of others." The truth is, however, that this limitation lies in the nature of freedom itself. Freedom is for powers of action; and a power implies resistance[11]—otherwise action is immediately at its goal—and resistance is a fundamental form of limitation.

The self-limitation of patterned action proper to the mature social being is not at all, as a rule, a compromise, a net loss of freedom; for the skater on a reasonably clear

11. *Consider what simple physical freedom without resistance would be like. If gravitation were eliminated, a muscular kick would project the body and the earth in opposite directions, with no return, and all further muscular action, ideally free, would reduce to futile wriggles in vacancy. Freedom made absolute commits suicide.*

sheet of ice, swift adjustment to the motions of other skaters heightens the enjoyment of skill. There is a primary inconsistency between complete satisfaction of physical impulses and complete satisfaction of social wishes; but the limitation on physical self-assertion required by social acceptability tends normally to heighten the value of physical experience. To this extent, the mature man is freer as limited than as unlimited; his self-limitation tends to coincide with the limitation which external power, acting in the common interest, would prescribe.

Thus civil law, which on its face is a restriction of our impulses, does in its total effect increase liberty. Men are less limited in solitude than in a dense society; but they are also less free for most of the significant objects of living. The hermit is free to sing, but not to sing in a chorus or an opera; and if he wants the social meaning of his own music, he wants all the rules which turn a medley of voices into a musical ensemble. If a man wants freedom to work for a long future, he wants to be free from the infinite friction of the incalculable, he has to know what he can expect from others; and, as a consequence, he wants a part of his own behavior like that of others to be curbed to a conventional pattern which will make prediction mutually possible—*he wants law*. It is true that the statutes, ordinances, traffic rules, and tax bills of any given society will contain much that is arbitrary or a heritage of unexamined custom: they will differ from anything which either his free fancy or his best intelligence could have schemed out for him; but at least they are *there* as working understandings between man and man, and they spare him the impossible task of thinking them out for himself! They inform him of the methods and costs of his freedom in that particular historical community. And he knows that he is in general freer there than in the forest.

But the chief limitation which lies in the nature of freedom itself is the limitation which all "equipment" imposes on the possessor. Material equipment is notoriously a bondage. But the equipment of mental and social powers is equally so, through the elementary requirements of technique. Thus the primary equipment of social impulses which we call "language" lays a costly demand on early mental efforts. The child must submit to a mass of arbitrary traditional linkages of vocal and visual signs with meanings as the price of his social negotiability. And all institutions,[12] which are in their nature social guides to certain freedoms, require the acceptance of a mold of action current in the given society.

The man who knows what he wants desires this degree of unfreedom as a means to the freedom which concerns him most, the freedom of his own peculiar talent within his society. It is the fool of modernity who supposes that freedom lies in liberation from the limitations of technique, and who, refusing the labor of the common language, makes himself unintelligible in the arts. The man of genuine ability wants another kind of freedom: freedom to take infinite pains, to spend infinite time, to be absolved from the demands of companionship and of bread and butter and the machinery of social obligation,

12. *"All institutions" seems too inclusive, unless this expression is taken in a strained sense. Slavery may be a guide to whatever freedoms it permits, but that is hardly its principal nature.*—CLARK.

68

in order that he may submit to the greater demands of his own subject matter. It is the glory of the modern state, on its freer side, that it allows individuals so great a gamut of choice in their field of limitation.

This means that freedom without limitation is a chimera. Concrete freedom is proportional not to the absence of rule but to the amount of rule it can absorb and turn into a ladder to achievement.

7. ACHIEVABLE FREEDOM

Agreeing that there is no unlimited freedom, and that the best brands of freedom need rules to grow on, it does not follow that every restriction is an aid to freedom. Every public order, simply because it promotes order, serves freedom to some extent; men are in general freer under a despotic regime which establishes firm law than in social chaos. But a public order may easily serve the orderer more than the ordered. Every existing social order, every inherited technique, every historical context with its cumulative wisdom is an instrument of liberty for which individuals will and do pay a great price; but in each case that price may be needlessly great. The choice is not between this heavy burden and chaos. The choice is between this heavy burden and a lighter burden which will serve the same ends.[13] Every such costly means of liberty is a fair target for criticism in behalf of a less costly and greater liberty.

The approach to perfect freedom, so far as it is achiev-

13. *The Hegelian argument that the state is an equipment for the liberty of its citizens is valid. Its implications become fallacious, because of the absence of the qualifications which we make here.*

able in human society, will follow no ideal of *least limitation;* it will, however, try to bring all social requirements, all restrictions by external agencies, into close agreement with what the growing reason of the individual would require of himself, under the given conditions of the community. In a community free to debate its own laws, the excessive, accidental, arbitrary, and obsolete tend to be peacefully discarded or replaced.

And through this liberty to try one's reason on the tough mass of unnecessary requirement, one learns a certain acceptance of the simple factual modeling of freedom which is one's "fate"—the nature of the physical world we live in, the oddities of our town, the defects of current social good sense which later generations may remove but not ours, the finitude of our own powers, the scantiness of time, the erratic human judgment of our work which strikes both over and under the mark of justice, the ever increasing demands of technical mastery which submerge today the free control we had won yesterday. In all these, the daily shapes of liberty, there is an element of chance and a lack of discernible justice in their historical apportionment; they outline the continuing task of liberty for each place and time.

But the most important freedom can always be had; that is, the freedom to perfect one's freedom. And to this end man requires a fairly complete liberty of his two powers of direct action (personal liberty) and the power of primitive social action (freedom of speech). These are not alone the necessary tools of any career which is not carried on in solitude; they are also necessary for the reshaping of the contours of freedom as it at any time exists. They are minimal and universal human demands.

Other freedoms are more subject to restriction through the levies they imply on the freedom of others.[14] Thus the ideal freedom to choose one's specialty, to work at the kind of job one likes, can be only partly satisfied in a finite society; for the free exercise of talent must not constrain those who do not wish its products. The ultimate satisfaction of the will, which is called "happiness," means in general that one's work is wanted or that one is valued for what he is if not for what he does; but freedom to pursue *this* happiness has no meaning except in a society of free spirits, liking what they like, and disliking what they dislike. Freedom to pursue happiness touches most immediately the ultimate freedom of others in their response; and the laws of success in this

14. *There is always a fringe of liberty, undefined in either law or morals, which finds sporadic voice in the disposition of humanity to turn wishes into rights. Thus we hear claims of a right of liberty to work or not to work, a right to privacy and to secretiveness, a right not to be pursued by reporters and photographers or to be shadowed by detectives or to have one's past life inquired into by prying neighbors, a right not to be candid-photographed or sketched by an artist of unknown intentions and abilities or caricatured whether in fun or in malice, a right to hear what one wishes to hear, including amateur and foreign music as against Mr. Petrillo, a right to be free from pressure to join things or to give to causes or to attend meetings, etc. The law has to decide when persistent appeal turns into persecution; where the right to know about people turns into invasion of privacy; where the freedom of the arts of portraying the human face clashes with the right to show one's features only where one wishes; and especially where the right to be informed impinges on the right of people, institutions, authorities, to withhold information. These dubious regions of liberty have a bearing on the obligations of the press, to be discussed.*

pursuit are not makable or alterable by any human society. All that society can control of the circumstances of the pursuit of happiness is (i) the liberty of appeal on the part of the pursuer (freedom of expression) and (ii) the liberty of the addressee to open or close his door to that appeal (personal liberty including the right of privacy).

8. THE RIGHT OF FREEDOM, AS ADDRESSED TO SOCIETY, IS NOT UNCONDITIONAL

An unconditional right is one whose claim no circumstance could alter, whatever the public emergency or whatever the state of will, honest or dishonest, just or malicious, of the person who claims it. In the Bill of Rights no conditions are attached verbally to the liberties there guaranteed; yet, as our practice, our statute law, our court decisions show, they are subject to at least one implied condition—that their exercise shall not threaten public security or good order. Arrest is a limited suspension of freedom; police power implies—under specified conditions—the possibility of arrest. There is no liberty (except the "freedom of thought" which society cannot reach) which even in the freest society may not be abridged at the demand of public safety. Legal rights are not unconditional.

But how about the underlying moral right of liberty which, with the rights of life and the pursuit of happiness, is by our tradition a birthright so firm that not even its possessors can alienate it?

The answer is that these fundamental human rights can be regarded as unconditional only if we refrain from giving reasons for them (as by calling them self-evident or axiomatic). If we give reasons for them—and there are reasons for our belief in them—those reasons state the condition on which the right is claimed. For if the facts proposed in the given reason are not present in any case, the ground for the claim in that case vanishes. This point is so obvious that it has generally escaped attention.

If, for example, a claim of right is supported on the ground of its social value or utility, then if its social value or utility should cease, the case for that claim of right would vanish. Any argument for liberty on the ground of the large balance of social advantage over social harm resulting from freedom—and this is the way I read the classic argument of John Stuart Mill—leaves the status of freedom sensitive to the question whether under any given circumstances—say, in time of extreme tension—this favorable balance persists. In Mill's opinion, the favorable balance is presumably so rooted in the nature of man and society that it could hardly be reversed; and any honest government would give liberty the benefit of the doubt. A totalitarian government, considering that free discussion had ceased to serve the public good, might in the same situation and by the same logic draw an opposite conclusion and suspend the right.

If the claim of right is made—as we have made it—on the basis of a nonpolitical duty of the individual, it could not be upset by a governmental disposition to question its momentary utility. But the claim of right is still conditional, because of the reason given for the right. If the claimant ignores or rejects his nonpolitical duty—as by using his liberty to disseminate falsehood, or to propagate for financial inducement views as his own which are not his own, or to distort for fees the true proportion of things (the essence of the perverse type of propaganda and "publicity")—the ground for his claim disappears. It belongs to the inner freedom of man that he may repudiate every ground on which he could rightfully claim civil freedom.

It may be reasonably doubted whether any man is, in fact, capable of an absolute and final rejection of duty. If the state continues to allow a man his life, it must also allow that the inner freedom which rejected duty remains as a possibility of rejecting the rejection. There is an element of freedom inseparable from human nature itself. But as addressed to society, a man may put an end to his own claim; in the absence of accepted moral duties, there are no moral rights. Hence, as addressed to society, there are *no unconditional rights.*[15]

The important turn of the present moment in our American theory of law, and indeed in all political theory, requires the recognition of this conditionality. We, and with us other societies aspiring to be free socie-

15. QUERY. *Does this mean that the place of a given right in the Bill of Rights is conditional, or only that the assignment of the right to an individual citizen should be regarded as subject to a condition?*—ANON.

—*The failure of an individual to meet the condition under which his claim of right is valid does not, of course, affect the position of the right in public policy, as long as the assumption of good will made by the recognition of right is valid for most citizens. It affects only that individual's own status in respect to the right. To make it clear to the individual that he may cancel his own claim by rejecting the duty that goes with the right is to limit his freedom for the sake of preserving the general freedom against inner decay, and hence, ultimately, the freedom of the abuser of freedom himself.*—W. E. H.

74

ties, have taken moral rights and the legal rights derived from them as unshakable claims; the word "unalienable" has added to the illusion that such a right cannot be forfeited. As a fighting creed, this position had its great work to do; there was a need for presenting human rights as fixtures which no state could remove because they were in the nature of things. But, since our community has achieved freedom from political tyranny, the need for limitation of the fighting absolute rights becomes evident.[16] Their advantage against the oppressor has now become the weakness of all liberal polities founded on them; for it has carried a claim that these fundamental rights are costless, that they are birthrights which impose no requirement on either disposition or conduct. Nursed on this milk, an arrogant type of individualism could arise, and not infrequently has arisen, sounding the "sacredness" of its unchallengeable privileges and making a mockery of free institutions. The time has

16. *I agree that a limitation becomes evident. I agree also with the general sense of this paragraph. In so far, however, as this and the preceding sentence refer to the rights named by Thomas Jefferson in the Declaration of Independence (and by their terms they seem to), I should like to dissent. The rights to life, to liberty, and to the pursuit of happiness are not conditional in the sense that there is a precondition to their exercise. And it is difficult to agree, in the light of the events of the past few years, that their historical work is done.*—MacLeish.

—*That we are "with the Declaration" will be evident from sec. 4, above, and the footnotes thereto. The historical work of the right of liberty will never be finished, so long as unfree states exist; but the claim of absoluteness has become a hindrance to that work. There is no precondition to the exercise of the fundamental rights; but there is the assumption of good will in their exercise, which it is possible for individual choice to cancel.*
—W. E. H.

come when the free state, if it is to have the vitality
fitting it for survival and the integrity of character which
can vindicate its principle to the broader world dubious
of "liberal" foundations, must cease to build its conceptions of liberty on assumptions radically contrary to fact,
as that rights are valid independent of the character of
the will that claims them. It must make clear that even
the "rights of man" rest on a condition of will; that only
the man who has his independent standard to serve,
and serves it, can justly call on the state to set limits to
its own freedom of action.

9. THE RIGHT TO GO WRONG

That a right is conditional does not mean that a claim
of right is canceled by error in its use. Human freedom
is freedom to experiment and, therefore, to go wrong.
Errors are part of the learning process. If society grants
a freedom, it knowingly accepts a degree of risk, a statistical probability of mistaken action; it accepts this as a
necessary price for an indispensable social good arising
from the undictated explorings of its individual members.

But what does cancel the ground of right is deliberate
or irresponsible going-wrong adopted as an individual
policy. Here the good will of the claimant, which is his
good faith with society, is purposely put aside; the resulting errors are not the tolerable errors incident to a
process of learning.

We say that the *ground* of right is canceled, not necessarily the legal right itself. The state of a person's will
is not visible; the law has to presume good faith, unless
there is tangible and persistent evidence to the con-

trary. Such tangible evidence is difficult to define and administer, as in all problems of intention or motivation in law. How and when the law has to take note of the loss of the ground of right we have later to inquire.[17] What concerns us at present is simply the crucial difference in principle between experimental mistake and the purposive exploiting of liberty.

But we must further note that if and when individual departures from good faith instead of being exceptional become generally prevalent, even the ordinary freedoms become unworkable, because the assumptions a free society makes in its grants of right are no longer in agreement with the dominant facts of public mentality. Mental alienation from the law, which may show itself in a hundred symptoms (such as the spread of black markets, undercover gang enterprise, and the like, but also in the politer forms of tax evasions, breaches of contract, the degradation of competitive or collective bargaining into private war, the cynical use of law by lawyers to beat the intent of law, etc.), may be in part the fault of the law and in part that vanishing of civic sense from the public mind which is the inward death of democracy; in any case, where such alienation exists, government must curb the abused liberty, reject the obnoxious law, or yield its place.

This means that the free society itself, though an unconditional goal, is not an unconditional good. It is not even intelligently safe under all circumstances. There may be, and at times have been, situations for the modern state in which it is not expedient either to withhold rights or to maintain them. Where the diversity of views,

17. See pp. 117–30.

the intensity of feeling, and the absence of over-all reflective judgment cancel the possibilities of a genuinely public discussion, as in certain later phases of the Weimar Republic, it is neither politically feasible to withdraw freedom of the press nor politically prudent to allow its persistent additions to the prevailing chaos of thought.

In sum, the growth of liberty in the modern state and its maintenance are dependent on an inner condition, a morale, which the state itself cannot create and most certainly cannot compel, but whose sources the state can learn, respect, and cultivate when they are present as the life of its system of rights. Whatever nourishes this morale nourishes the entire system; whatever depresses this morale or denatures it into a cunning utility saps the veins of all freedom. In its nature this morale itself is either free or nonexistent; it was by a true instinct that in the history of Europe it is the freedom of conscience for which modern man first showed himself willing to die.

3

FREEDOM OF THE PRESS AS FREEDOM FOR SPEAKERS

WHATEVER experience has taught us about freedom in general will hold good for freedom of the press. But freedom of the press has its own life and history; it will more than pay its debt by the substance it returns to our total sense of human liberty. We consider it now on its own merits, but not without reference to its intimate companion in our social outlook, freedom of speech.

10. FREEDOM OF PRESS AND FREEDOM OF SPEECH: LIKENESSES AND DIFFERENCES

With good reason, freedom of the press is commonly bracketed with freedom of speech. The phrase "freedom of expression" may include them both. Their functions merge into each other. Speech, as its audience grows, becomes a species of mass communication. "Freedom of speech" has always meant more than freedom of private conversation (which tyrannies have often desired to suppress and have sometimes succeeded in driving to whispers and furtive sign language, but whose traceless body, almost ghostly in nature, eludes every control); it has meant freedom to address groups and assemblies, to practice the arts of persuasion, to teach, to exhort, to urge public action—in a hundred ways to "publish" one's views. The press at first does hardly more than implement this natural activity with means for reaching a more extended audience in space and, through the durability of print, in time. Today, the voice, by the aid of radio, has overtaken the scope of print as well as surpassing its speed; so again the town crier proclaims his news reports and his opinions by word of mouth, but now to the nation. There is good reason, therefore, to think of these two modes of expression as similar in point of principle; their groundwork appears identical. That all men ought to be free to say what they want to say leads us to argue by analogy that all men ought to be free to print what they want to print, within the same bounds of good citizenship and common decency.

This analogy cannot be fully trusted, however, without observing that there are important differences between speech and press. Are they such as to affect the nature of the freedom?

Speech is a natural function of the human being, the breath of his social life; it requires no external apparatus. The press is an institution of an advanced civilization, a machine-using institution, whose scope and technique become more extensive as new instruments are devised. It has extended many fold the natural working environment of personal life—one's daily business may be affected by market or news reports from across oceans. It has made possible the political unity of large states, and without its aid the incipient order of mankind would be inconceivable. For these increasing services the press has created an answering appetite; and whatever problems it faces today are largely the problems due to its achievements. Almost we may say that the press has altered human nature by making it second nature for man to live in the enlarged world which it alone makes mentally visible.

It might seem, then, that while freedom of speech is a universal claim, as belonging to human nature, freedom of the press as an artificial activity would be a claim limited to those who own or use its instruments. This apparent difference is reinforced by the fact that, from the first, speech and printed thought have a different impact upon the recipient. The relative impersonality of the printed word, its permanence, the considerable apparatus required to produce it, the inability to conceal or recall what has once become printed record—all these suggest a deeper conviction, a stronger sense of importance, and a more careful responsibility of statement on the part of the issuer, and thus convey an intimation of authority which may or may not correspond with the true inwardness of the source. The sophisticated public of today has by no means outgrown the feeling that what comes "in black and white" must be more of a *credendum* than what falls perishably on the ear.[1] This stronger bid for belief is enhanced by the circumstance that to what is printed there is no immediate reply and that not so many can print as can talk. For these reasons—while no one is prohibited from owning a press—it has tended to become the medium of expression for a minority. In a lesser degree than the pulpit, the desk, or the rostrum, but equally in principle, the press is in practice the voice of a specialized group, one whose business it is to *know*. To know,

1. *The difference between the law of libel and the law of slander is instructive here.*—HUTCHINS.

not indeed in the sense of scientific analysis, but in the sense of awareness of event, of intelligence of observation which nothing significant escapes and nothing merely trivial detains, of being "in the know" of the behind-scene play of personalities and interests, able to sleuth out what someone has called the "lowdown of the lowdown"—an ideal, one might think, making infinite requisitions upon sophistication if not on sagacity. And while disillusionment regarding fine appearances would be a good, indeed a necessary preliminary training, it might also require for perfection disillusion with disillusion, so that occasionally the good newsman would be saved for admitting the existence of simplicity, integrity, and beauty of spirit and happily freed from being "the dupe of his own distrust." He must be the kind of realist who knows and sees the reality of the ideal. These qualifications are high; they are moral as well as mental. No one can know enough, nor be enough, to be a perfect reporter of event.

Conversation may become an art; it can never be a profession. No one, I suspect, regards it as his or her chief vocation. But the work of the press is at least a vocation. It brings conversation nearest the character at once of a profession and an art; it brings a professional quality nearest the human continuity of conversation. Its genius is the infinite improvisational artistry of perceiving and capturing in swift strokes the element of "story" in the tangled and perishing human scene. The reporter has thought of himself too exclusively under the figure of the detective or of the connoisseur; let him think of himself more as the poet disguised in the crowd, responsive to all its qualities, not excluding the secret dignity and "glory of the imperfect."

Whether or not the pertinent qualifications for press excellence can be defined and put into requirements of law or custom, the public instinctively ascribes special skills to one who has come so far as to get his script "into the papers." He has now a special function; he is set apart. Is this a superstition which should be overcome or a recognition to be made more definite?

The answer to this question will depend less on whether special skill is actually required for good work by the press—which will hardly be questioned—than on the importance of the service which it renders to consumers. If, as in the other professions—law, teaching, the ministry—these services are of grave concern at once to their users and to the community, calling both for a technique and for an ethics, specialization and specialized training should have a new emphasis and greater recognition. The reverse side of the picture, the disservice which incompetence armed with the present instruments of communication can inflict on the consumer, might well add to the doubt whether freedom of the press means or should mean freedom to all on equal terms to use the powers of the press without so much as an automobile license. It would surely be fallacious to argue that if any man ought to be able to speak to his neighbor, he ought by that same sign to be free to speak to an indefinite number of neighbors or to the nation, on any subject matter, and in any state of temper whatever. It is simply not plausible that hasty judgments conveyed with the eloquence of high emotion and permissible to a Hyde Park iconoclast can be regarded with the same friendly impassivity when they can reach instantly a large proportion of the citizens of a modern state.

The scope of the press has not only increased absolutely; it has multiplied in proportion to that of all other agencies of expression. The family can still reach only its own; the schools only their appropriate generation; the churches only those who are disposed to attend; but the press, including, we recall, radio and film, can reach all, without limit of consanguinity or building space or entrance examination or age group or type of faith, without delay or by your leave. It is at least an open question, under these circumstances, whether the quantitative impact of the present-day media of mass communication does not create a qualitative change in the problem of untrammeled press freedom which it would be both foolish and uncandid not to examine.

We propose to examine it. But, for the present, we shall as far as possible leave the consumer, and therefore these complications, out of the picture. We shall treat freedom of the press as what the phrase on its face implies, an individual freedom concerning nobody but the man who has something he wants to say through a mass medium to a mass audience. The case of the consumer and his interests, as reacting on this freedom to express, we shall deal with in our fifth chapter.

Considering the press, then, solely as a means of expression for the expresser, we must hold that the mechanism of approach of the speaker to his audience does not *of itself* affect the moral or legal position of his claim to freedom. Every tool is, in its nature, an extension of the human body. The tools of communication are quite as much in the line of growth of our natural speech as the automobile is in the line of growth of our natural locomotion. If telephone and telegraph, as facilities for enlarging the range of speech, should be open to all on equal terms, so by whatever instrument at any time man is able to reach an audience, through print or radio, through film or television, it would seem just that every man, under reasonable conditions,[2] should be able to gain access to its use, provided always that the ancient and eternal liberty of the addressee not to listen and not to read remains intact.

On this point, we have to remember that, in our time, it is often harder to escape from the voice than from the printed word, which is incapable of physical aggression. While print has its peculiar force, speech has advantages of its own. The printed word is not only silent; it moves its readers toward solitude. When the family newspapers come, conversation ceases, and the group dissolves into a set of submerged individuals. One inclines to run away with magazine or book as a dog with his bone. The magnetism of the speaker is absent; the stir of the audience, the companionship of emotion, the instant rapport and response between speakers and hearers, the invention of ideas and the creation of mood that occurs—all these are lacking to the eye-and-paper fixation. Attempting to recover for reading some of the animation and sociability of living speech, reading aloud to a group is a partial union of both (for many, a laborious and unnatural exertion). And, when the crisis of a political campaign is at hand, no political party will trust its fortunes to the sober reasoning of printed words; it must

2. *Among which the natural limitations of the medium, such as radio, are obviously to be included.*

bring its candidates forward in person; they must have or acquire a "radio voice," or at least be able to produce a victrola record which can be blared to the helpless crowds through loud-speakers as a sad substitute for the almost physical lift with which man speaking sways his hearers. Einstein, thinking of a campaign to excite realization of the atomic age, has said, "Merely reading about the bomb promotes knowledge in the mind, but only talk between men promotes feeling in the heart." This partly interchangeable and yet partly supplementary character of the two media indicates the antecedent implausibility of finding a line of principle between them.

As to universality, if freedom of speech is a universal liberty, and if it carries over without change into the new era with all its new capacity for penetrating and limitless assault, it is not at once clear that prospective freedom to use the press should be less universal, though the question of right has still to be raised. In point of fact, the use of the press today is by no means limited to the few who own presses or whose vocation it is to contribute to them. Every local paper has indeed its owner; but to whom does its space belong? In large part, to a swarm of social interests whose doings demand due publicity on pain of group wrath if it is not forthcoming. Those who require more may pay for space or submit a letter. And while the great machines of mass communication have grown increasingly costly and complex, there has been at the same time a cheapening of the elementary and publicly available press instruments. There is no one who, in a pinch, cannot mimeograph a manifesto or throw a handbill or phototype a pamphlet. Moving between the opposite impossibilities of giving full vent to every voice inspired to address the public, and giving vent to no voice at all but that of its owners, the contemporary press does, with some success, bring forward a sample of the public to address the public. Whether it is a fair sample, and whether there are better modes of selection, and by what standards, we have to inquire.

And especially the problem is before us in what sense freedom of the press is a right.

We shall open that question, as we did the question of liberty in the broad, by asking what the actual working value of free expression is, first for the individual and then for the community. The value is not the right; but, were it not for the value, no one would care to claim the right.

11. THE VALUE OF FREE EXPRESSION

For the speaker unimpeded utterance has three radical values. First of all, as the circulating medium of the stream of social consciousness, speech requires no ulterior aim to justify its existence. It may be a mere hello, a shrug, or a series of casual feelers thrown out from personal solitude to test, like a set of soundings, the temper of the social medium. In this primitive capacity free expression has a value independent of anything said; it is the value of maintaining mutual awareness, which is the elementary life-process of the social being.

But speech also has a purpose of its own, commonly described as the "conveying of ideas," i.e., the exchange of information, the transmission of feeling and judgment, the reciprocal answering of questions—in brief, a give-and-take of individual items of mental trade. From this point of view, men require freedom of speech not because they require to emit opinions, but because they require to receive from others what their speech conveys, and they can get it only by exchange. Free speech, on this showing, is a sort of domestic enterprise occupied with traffic in an indispensable commodity, ideas.

While this is a genuine aspect of the value of speech, it is not the most significant aspect. If an idea is born in a man, it is not an item of capital stock; he has an impulse to give it away, to spread it everywhere in the knowledge that what he gives he keeps. He is not satisfied with "expression"; he desires to secure for his idea current acceptance; he works to promote it; he argues for it as for a child—it *is* his offspring. His concern for it belongs to the deepest instinct of his nature, that which Nietzsche called the will to power, and Plato the desire for immortality; let Plato and Nietzsche correct each other, and let us call this instinct the will to power *through ideas*. This impulse is akin to the reproductive impulse; it is the instinct for mental self-propagation. To be unfree to speak is to be thwarted of one's spiritual children. The family is the first and necessary field for the transmission of one's mental self; it is a factor in "social heredity." But an idea defines its own scope; it is usually destined for the wider community: man's normal will to power through ideas leads him to seek for them what we call "influence." The destiny of private thought is to gain power and effect through shaping public behavior or public enactment. Nothing could more describe a human failure than a man physically prolific whose ideas should count for nothing to his group or his time. A suppression of speech, in its most painful consequence, would be the mental sterilization of the community.

And with this would occur the stunting of thought. It is true that thinking as a mental process is inherently free and inaccessible to external control. Yet it is idle to say that freedom of thought remains when the expression of thought is restrained through the fear of penalty. The private process of thinking is not complete without its outside circuit, the interaction of its expression with the aroused responses. The maxim, "Think before you speak," is fair enough as a check upon unconsidered loquacity, but it overlooks the great extent to which men normally use conversation as a part of their thinking process; they think by way of speaking. A stoppage of expression, therefore, tends to bring about an atrophy of thinking itself.

In all these ways free expression is necessary to individual mental existence on the human level.

12. THE SOCIAL VALUE OF FREE EXPRESSION

The primitive social interest in free expression is simply that, without expression, there is no society. Communication is the stuff of social life; that life is full in proportion to the unhampered normality of individual expression.[3] Here the social value of freedom has its

3. *In the interest of realism it is pertinent to remark at this point that there is such a thing as a too expressive, too loquacious, too unreticent society, taking out in endless talk what a soberer guard at the lips would reduce to relevant and sincere discourse. The liberal tradition has taken a too quantitative view of the virtues of speech; and the time is not far away when humanity*

clearest illustration; society has no other intelligence, no other fertility, no other raw material of advance than what individuals spontaneously give out from their own minds through acts of expression. Inventiveness, essential to preservation under new conditions, cannot be commanded. If society attempts to determine what shall be uttered, it has no criterion except the old stock already in hand to recognize what is useful in the new product; its vital novelty must come from the uncontrollable spontaneity of individual mental gestation. Any process of control which rebukes this spontaneity endangers the future social vitality.

One radical difference, however, between physical gestation and mental gestation is that in physiological reproduction the percentage of defective infants is very small; in mental gestation, very high. The number of worthless and unviable ideas begotten by human minds is prodigious. The normal give-and-take of society is the natural method for securing the necessary infant mortality of the unfit. Friendship is—among other things—a social instrument for the euthanasia of ill-begotten ideas; it is highly efficient because the atmosphere of friendship is tolerant, and, while certain ideas are remolded, sometimes actually reborn, to fit them for a public career, many are quietly and painlessly snuffed out in the course of a courteous hearing. The act of expression is often sufficient to enable the fond parent to see his folly, through gaining for the first time an objective view of his offspring. Quite a number get through

will revolt against the flood of blab and print. But we are concerned here with the positive and far the most important aspect of the case.

into the world of current talk, appear in the papers, and fade away of themselves. Relatively few reach the arena of the hard struggle for survival. This spontaneous social process of selection is so efficient that no agency consciously controlled and supervised could begin to compare with it. If we were to put up a case for the right of free speech solely on the ground of its social utility, we should certainly do well to cite the beautiful and frictionless quietude with which this necessary elimination of folly proceeds.

13. THE TRADITIONAL ARGUMENT FOR FREE SPEECH AND FREE PRESS

Free expression has commonly been recommended both to social tolerance and to legal protection on the ground of its utility; and especially on the ground of the tendency of the mature free discussion of the ultimate public forum to yield truth, or a better brand of truth than could otherwise become available. This argument ascribes a high selective efficiency to those encounters of ideas in the public forum which are subsequent to the processes of early weeding-out described above.

From Milton onward the plea for free speech and press has appealed to a tendency of free competition among ideas to bring about ascendency of the best. Milton takes his famous image of Truth "in open encounter with Error" from the jousting meet. Justice Holmes finds his analogy in the market place, no doubt with a reminiscent glance toward Adam Smith's analysis of the processes of free competitive bargaining which recommends laissez faire. In either case, the figures suggest that freedom and variety of the entries, as well as freedom in the contest itself, favor the validity of the resulting choice. As Judge Learned Hand has put it, our First Amendment "presupposes that right conclusions are more likely to be gathered out of a multitude of tongues than through any kind of authoritative selection."

Unhappily, none of the analogies used in these arguments corresponds too closely to the actualities of what we euphemistically call "public debate." The jousters in the tourney field made a point of meeting one another, and something had to give way. But in the free spate of opinions by the many organs of press utterance in the contemporary scene, there is no assurance that idea will encounter idea in any genuine contest. How many readers among the millions try systematically to invite into their minds views critical of their preferred source of enlightenment? How many editors, holding divergent views of serious public questions, cite each other to open debate; what Hearst has flung the gauntlet down to what *New York Times*—or vice versa?

The market-place figure is still less apposite. In the market place the buyer is on his guard; he has time to compare, he can sample and test the quality of his purchase; and the sellers, to gain customers, have to try to do better each one than his best rival; the "higgling of the market" jostles prices to a "reasonable" level. But where in the market place of ideas do the buyers sample and compare the offerings; and what are their tests of quality? Does not an idea present itself as its own test of quality? In the hurly-burly of competing voices of the press, the buyers seeking what is congenial to their existing views tend rather to avoid what would expose defects. Adam Smith's plea for a free market was based on the doctrine that "man is led by an invisible hand to promote an end which is no part of his intention." But in public debate if no individual intends the common good of truth, no invisible hand can educe truth from their mélange of proffered plausibilities. I fear it is simply not the case that in the profuse and unordered public expression of today the best views tend to prevail.

It is true that flagrant error tends to be shown up in time and to be replaced by something less bad. It is also true that individuals who know the art and the cost of finding truth will be aided by the wealth and diversity of suggestions thrown out upon the current flood, provided they are equipped with a sturdy capacity to discard an immense mass not worth the pain of investigation and to look for themselves behind what is published. Whatever is "the best truth," it is not tagged for general recognition; and the man who would like to back Truth as the winner has first to determine what it is. In most cases, it is not one of the contestants at all, but something through them and among them which has to be laboriously identified. And when some portion of it has been discovered, the finder has still to labor—not always through throwing it back into public competition—to put it at public disposal. The classical argument is not sustained by an examination of current facts.

How public opinion is at any time actually formed demands analysis. For the most part, the voluminous tangle of expression has no "result"; nor has the total efflux of the press a structure which entitles it to the name of a "discussion." The coexistence of an unlimited variety of opinion is not equivalent to debate. Nor has our public mêlée of voices any hopper out of which "results" emerge, like clean oats from a thresher. A partial organization of the medley of voices is induced for political purposes by inserting into the scene at a specified future date a Ballot, indicating that at that time a public Decision must be reached. The intervening time is full—not of debate between candidates—but of Able Utterances by them, across each other, into the public resonance chamber, plus much nonpublic Group-Bargaining addressed not to Thinkers but to competent Bread-butterers who will also resolutely ply the ballot box; out of this mixed process will issue the "Verdict of the People." From the total agitation something is gained; some sharpened awareness of current issues, some added distrust of the party-painted versions of truth, some showing-up of pretense, much crowd emotion and underneath it a modicum of quiet individual reflection, at last a mass resolve representing a vague balance of impression in the mass sensorium—an intuition whose direction may or may not be just. As a process of public thinking, it lacks structure as much as it lacks integrity. Public discussion, of which this process is a semblance, is a necessary condition of a free community; and freedom of expression is a necessary condition of an amply furnished public discussion. Without something of the kind no self-governing society could operate. But in neither case is the necessary condition *sufficient*.

What the existing process does achieve is to elicit mental power and breadth in those participants whom it does not baffle or confuse. As long as the will to find truth is undiscouraged and lively, free expression tends to produce a stronger and more self-conscious citizenship. It is less its truth product than its human product which we can count on.

A socially authoritative control of the allowable contents of the public idea pool might save the mind from confusion, but at the cost of also saving it from the arduous effort to reach valid judgments; it would tend to deprive society of à citizenship prepared to fend off illusions and shams through its experience of their nature. The virility of this human product, I repeat, is the great social value of free expression. And if it can be shown that this virility can be preserved by pure laissez faire and only by laissez faire, society would have a strong ground for maintaining it.

The true antithesis to "authoritative control," however, is not unaided and unguided individual truth-seeking; it is individual truth-seeking with the aid of "free authorities" such as normally exist in every society, serving to clarify without coercion the complex business of individual judgment.

It may not be superfluous to say that the "authoritative control" which is here set in antithesis to free expression is not the normal authority, essential in a free society as in all society, to the clarification of living. The authoritative shelter of the family protects the early stages of mental growth from an intolerable aimlessness and provides certain vital hypotheses for later critical examination. The authority of science by a necessary mental division of labor replaces an impossible alternative, a demand upon each citizen to recapitulate through his own laboratory work the scientific experience of the race. The authority of religion provides stable points of reference for the wider issues of life, leaving every individual free to develop his own philosophy and promote it, without losing sight of his bearings on the original chart. The looser authorities of custom and the institutions, economic and other, provide presumptive but not prescriptive routes to the major human satisfactions. These authorities are to be distinguished as "free authorities" just in so far as they renounce the instruments of social coercion. And in this free condition, instead of limitations of freedom, they are means to freedom; they are the equipment for a more concrete freedom than could be had without them. It would be a starved and barren pioneering which should attempt to dispense with all authority. The art of living is to know how to use the authorities and to remain free with them.

When these free authorities are weak or absent, the weaker truth-seekers may so far flounder as to set up a prima facie case for a reversion to authoritative control, to the loss of that mental power on which social progress depends. Under normal circumstances the social value of free expression is sufficient to justify its protection as a public policy, though not as an individual right.

14. FREE EXPRESSION AS A RIGHT

Whatever is so intimately bound up with mental existence and normal growth as expression is may reasonably be regarded as a part of that freedom which a man not only does claim as an interest but ought to claim as a right, for himself and also for others. It has an aspect of duty and therefore has a different status from that of a personal desire or a privilege granted by society for social ends.

Neither the value nor the duty of expression is limited to its more purposeful aspects. Speech and press may be trivial, casual, emotional, amusing, imaginative, speculative, whimsical, foolish; all utterance serves a social end—to report to fellow-beings mutual presence and interest, the play of mood, the vagaries of taste, the gropings for principle, the barometric flux of belief and disbelief, hope and fear, love and hate, and thus to shape attitudes which emerge in group feeling and action. Through an untrammeled utterance meeting an equally untrammeled response, including such anger or contempt as the utterance may arouse, men discover their own wills and tastes, find confirmation or rebuke, mold their own growth and that of others. Expression is an experimental prelude of action: it is the explorative mid-world between thought and the commitment of deed; it is a growth function for all mental creation. There is, I believe, a common duty to protect the whole range of this freedom, as a right of social existence.

But, in a more special sense, the expression of thought is an individual duty. If a man is burdened with an idea, he not only desires to express it; he ought to express it. The socially indispensable function of criticism may be as abhorrent to the diffident as it is attractive to the self-confident or pugnacious; but for neither is the issue one of wish. It is one of obligation—to the neighbor, to the community, and also to what is beyond the community— let us say, to truth. It is the duty of the scientist or the discoverer to his result, of Confucius to his teaching, of

Socrates to his oracle. It is the duty of every man to his belief. It is not limited to special persons and special occasions; it has a certain totality. The life-task of everybody includes an effort to give currency to his unique view of things, which in so far as it is or contains truth has the quality of universality. For many a man this is the greater part of that task. In any case, one's relation to what he himself *sees* constitutes for him a major obligation, and the freedom of expression here merges with freedom of conscience.

Because of this duty to what is beyond the state, freedom of speech and freedom of press are moral rights which the addressee must respect, even if that addressee be the state itself.

This duty of the individual thinker to his thought is the original source of supply for the process of public debate whose value for the community we have examined; it is fitting that the primary ground of the individual's right should be rather at the source than at the outcome of this process.

While it is not, like the right of speech, a universal right that every citizen should own a press or be an editor or have access to the clientele of any existing press, it is the whole point of a free press that ideas deserving a public hearing shall get a public hearing and that the decision of what ideas deserve that hearing shall rest in part with the public, not solely with the particular biases of editors and owners. In any populous community a vigorous trimming-out process among ideas presenting themselves for wide public hearing is obviously essential; but freedom of the press becomes a mockery unless this selective process is free also. This means that free speech, with its informal emphases, is the natural vestibule to a free press and that the circumstance of ownership of press instruments confers no privilege[4] of deafness toward ideas which the normal selective processes of the community promote to general attention.

15. THE RIGHT OF FREE EXPRESSION
REQUIRES PROTECTION

This is true because ideas are neither separate objects, nor passive objects, nor indifferent objects; but by their nature they at once interlock with other ideas and not infrequently lock horns. Human beings in free motion may or may not collide; ideas in motion necessarily col-

4. *On the contrary, it may impose a duty. Freedom of the press is a right belonging, like all rights in a democracy, to all the people. As a practical matter, however, it can be exercised only by those who have effective access to the press. Where financial, economic, and technological conditions limit such access to a small minority, the exercise of that right by that minority takes on fiduciary or quasi-fiduciary characteristics. The exclusive exercise of a general right by a limited minority can be justified only if the exercise is of such a character as to realize the general purpose for which the right was established. One of the purposes of the guaranty of freedom of the press was to assure the publication of the widest possible variety of opinion.—*MacLeish.

*—The fiduciary implications of the minority use of the press are important. This is adverted to again, at p. 153, below. I doubt the strict analogy between the universality of the right of freedom of the press and that of freedom of speech, for reasons given in part above (opening of chap. 3). But also because freedom of speech seems to me less on a footing with freedom of the press than a natural preparation for an artificial sequel; the universality appropriate to the press can only be in the base of selection, not in the exercise. It must be in nobody's power to exclude anybody from entering the lists which may bring him, through fair testing, to the use of the mass media.—*W. E. H.

lide, in the sense of coming to terms with other extant ideas. To say that they are "understood" is to say that they find their relationship, harmonious or discordant, in the world of living ideas and therefore in the world of facts. The notion of an idea as an innocent and pacific entity is an illusion foisted on thought by language. The word—especially the printed word—is separable, quiescent, submissive; the idea it stands for is an unlimited intrusion, aggressive and unyielding, into the whole system of thought and action. The utterance of opinion is not merely the announcement of an "I think. . . . ." It is a social force and is intended so to be.

Since civilized society is a working system of ideas, it lives and changes by the ingestion of ideas. It is vulnerable to every shock to the fortunes of the ideas it embodies. And since there is usually less motive for uttering ideas with which everybody and every institution is in accord than in uttering those destined to change men's minds, a significant idea will be likely to arouse resistance roughly proportionate to its value. (This is not the same as to say that the resistance aroused by an idea is a guaranty of its worth.) The issuer of ideas will have need of protection—but of what protection?

Freedom of expression can never be made a costless immunity by shackling hostile response, even if it were desirable to do so. For response is also expression. Free expression is destined to liberate social conflict, not to repress it. It should mean, however, that *the level of social conflict is lifted from the plane of violence to the plane of discussion.* It should mean to the issuer that he is protected—not from anger, contempt, suffering, the loss of his clientele, for in this case his critic would be unfree—but from types of harm *not an integral part of the argument or relevant to the argument* (wrecking the issuer's shop, threatening his employees, intimidating his patrons, etc.).

There are those who would define freedom of expression as meaning no pain and no opprobrium to the issuer, no matter what he proposes. This ideal, if it is such, could be realized only in a society to which all ideas had become either impotent or indifferent. In any actual and mentally lively society free speech will always require courage. And the first danger to free expression will always be the danger at the source, the timidity of the issuer, or his purchasability.

a) The effective agencies for protecting free expression are the community and the government.—The community acts, first by routing social conflict through the ballot box, encouraging the method of discussion by making it a preliminary to action, and, then, by such traditions of self-restraint and toleration as may exist.

But, in the steadiest of communities, the struggle among ideas tends to become physical as it becomes prolonged; there is an incessant downtrend of debate toward the irrelevant exchange of punishments—malicious pressures, threats and bribes, broken windows and broken heads. Government is the only agency which, through its monopoly of physical force, can measurably insure that argument in speech and press will continue to be argument and not competitive injury. The elementary function of government in simply maintaining public order and the rights of person and property must be noted as the cornerstone of free expression, inasmuch as the cruder menaces to freedom are always from within the community.

Wherever in society there is an institution, a body of belief or interest, an organized power—good, bad, or mixed—there is a potential (we do not say actual) foe of the free critic—good, bad, or mixed. This potential hostility to the challenger is due not simply to the fact that it is easier and more natural for the obstinate vein in human nature to discourage or repress the critic than to meet his argument. Since the critic of established things has the uphill task, it is the tendency of our instinctive sympathy with the underdog to dramatize his struggle as one of courageous light against intrenched darkness. Our argument should assume this, but still the defender of the established order may be justified in suspecting some few elements of the Old Adam both in the attacker and in the audience he collects and stirs. The utterance of criticism is seldom an appeal to pure reason empty of emotion; and the public remonstrance which he intends to arouse is not necessarily in the temper of a Socratic dialogue; its quality depends on the intelligence, the prejudice, the emotional boiling-points of the consumer.[5] Freedom of the press to appeal to reason is liable to be taken as freedom to appeal to public passion, ignorance, vulgarity, cynicism. Or, to put it conversely, wherever fraud or malicious mischief is afloat through the press, or an intent to break over the bounds of decency for a profit, there at a whisper of protest the cry is sure to be raised that "freedom of the press is in danger." We dare not burke the fact that freedom of the

5. A matter which deserves far more attention than the liberal argument has given it and to which we revert in our final section.

press is dangerous, not so much in itself as in elements of mental and emotional instability in its public sounding-board; and that those who incline to mute the critic have a case. But supposing the worst of the critic; suppose his motive bad and his argument worse: there is no cure for him or his argument in refusing to argue or in repressing him. In so far as he has caught the attention of a part of the public, there is no substitute for the patient attempt to reach the element of reasonableness in the public mind, *as long as the belief can be kept that a lurking reasonableness is there.* This lurking reasonableness is what we have referred to earlier as the Socratic element in the mind of the people which differentiate them from the "masses" of Ortega y Gasset.[6] Suppression of the critic implies loss of faith in the residual good sense and good will of the public. The hope for democracy lies in the possibility of maintaining that faith and, because of that, of maintaining the critic's freedom. If the existing centers of social power are hesitant in their confidence in public reason, if they are convinced by experience or by the teachings of certain current phases of psychology that the ultimate springs of human conduct are irrational and that in the mass mankind is even more irrational than in the individual package, one can at least understand a disposition on their part to restrain or to exert irrelevant pressures upon the utterance of critical opinion. Because the democratic faith cannot be compelled,[7] these existing centers of social power

6. Above, p. 46.

7. *And because, as I would personally be inclined to point out, the main trend of scientific psychology spread through and by our higher learning is unwittingly against democracy, purely on*

are at any time the chief potential menaces to press freedom.

And the first line of defense for press freedom is government, so far as it is able and disposed to maintain order and personal security and to exercise in behalf of press freedom the elementary sanctions against sabotage, blackmail, and corruption.

b) Government as protecting freedom against government.—Any power capable of protecting freedom is also capable of infringing freedom. This is true both of the community and of government. In modern society the policy of government vis-à-vis the free expression of its citizens is in peculiar need of definition.

For every modern government, liberal or otherwise, has a specific position in the field of ideas; its stability is vulnerable to critics in proportion to their ability and persuasiveness. To this rule, a government resting on popular suffrage is no exception. On the contrary, just to the extent that public opinion is a factor in the tenure and livelihood of officials and parties, such a government has its own peculiar form of temptation to manage the ideas and images entering public debate.

The reality of press freedom, therefore, depends on the will of the people to set limits upon the capacity of government to interfere with, regulate, control, or suppress the voices of the press, or to manipulate the data on which public judgment is formed.

---

the ground mentioned, that man's fundamental being is commonly declared as a scientifically confirmed truth to have an impulsive and nonrational basis. No people which accepts the belief that intellect is a creature of impulsive or subconscious or material or economic necessities can possibly maintain a democratic faith in the reasonableness of the common man or, by inference, in the institution of a free press.

Such self-limitation of the state cannot be contrary to the public interest. For, as a condition under which men reach their highest mental power and character, free expression offers a long-range service to the community against which no state could move without moving against itself. Further, whatever its judgment of the opinions expressed, no nation can have a net or long-time interest in repressing the conscience of its citizens, if and when conscience dictates expression of opinion. It is the peculiarity of the modern state that it has become aware of this fact and has begun to recognize the citizen's conscience as one source of its own vitality. This is the strong position of the right of free expression vis-à-vis society, that it requires no moment-to-moment justification in terms of other services to society than these intrinsic and indispensable services; its claim is not therefore withdrawable at the discretion of any representative of the social will to whom it may appear that *other* social ends, such as present content and prosperity or support of the existing regime, are not being served.

There are obligations of the state to security and public order which may oblige it to limit free expression under special circumstances.[8] But, even when this is the case, the action of government has a self-stultifying quality; for if public thinking is bedeviled and confused, the root of trouble is not met by choking the utterance of private thought. Private thinking itself cannot be suppressed, nor does silencing it put any other view—least of all the government's view—in its place; the private thinking process may be starved or suffocated, but the effort to suppress its output accentuates its motive force.

8. See below, sec. 20 and chap. 4.

As a matter of plain political expediency, nothing more stimulates the inventiveness of evasion, and nothing more clamors for speedy removal, than an unaccustomed clamp placed on natural freedom of speech and press.

The essential position is that the citizen's relation to his truth must remain more imperative to him than his relation to any state or social order; otherwise—and this is the paradox—he cannot be a fit citizen or member of society. Unless he can serve his society with his truth, all his other service is corrupted at its source.

This is the basis of the First Amendment. It is the basis also of Milton's just estimate that the right of free speech (which for him was also freedom of the press) is "above all rights."

16. THE RIGHT OF FREE SPEECH AND PRESS MUST INCLUDE THE RIGHT TO BE IN ERROR

Otherwise, discussion could not exist, and persuasion would have no work to do. This right therefore implies toleration of error, and this is its chief working edge. In order that the man who is right but is supposed to be wrong may continue to state his views, the man who is wrong but thinks himself right must be allowed to do the same.

It is important for our purpose to observe that toleration does not mean laziness, indifference, or an abandonment of confidence that truth can be known. Here the classical defenders of freedom risk transmitting with their pleas certain gracious poisons; as the opposite of total dogmatism they suggest a total incertitude. One of Mill's main reasons for accepting the expression of apparent error is that it may, after all, be right; he is here renewing Milton's warning that if we attempt to prohibit at all, "nothing is more likely to be prohibited than the truth itself." This argument, taken at face value, carries a decent human modesty about our convictions to the point of implying that we do not know the truth when we see it. But if this is the case, Milton's fine picture of Truth and Falsehood in free and open encounter loses its point; for, to know whether or not Truth is ever "put to the worse," one must be able during the combat to identify Truth. If his only test of Truth were that often-quoted dictum of Mr. Justice Holmes, "The best test of truth is the power of thought to get itself accepted in the competition of the market," then no one knows which is Truth until the fight is over. In which case, Milton has said exactly nothing; the winner always wins.

This is certainly not Milton's intention, and probably not that of Holmes. For it would have an additional disadvantage, unwelcome to either of these robust spirits, that until the battle was over no one could know on which side to join the fight! If we are caught in a complete antecedent incertitude or relativity of our minds in respect to truth, we must indeed be tolerant, but we reduce ourselves to bystanders in the struggle, we cease to fight, and free speech loses all interest in persuasion and all importance. The alternative is that some truth at least must be knowable in advance, and toleration must be the toleration of error which we know to be such.

It is of course the case that "it belongs to the human condition to be commonly in quest of truth rather than in possession of it." When we are consciously in this usual situation, toleration is not called for, because there is no disposition to intolerance; the search for truth becomes a joint inquiry along different lines of hypothesis. Toleration is only called for when we feel ourselves in presence of error, and in possession together with others of the relevant bit of truth, and when that truth seems important. The fact that this feeling may be mistaken does not cancel the possibility that it may be valid. It is this possibility which makes the contest with error significant and terminable. Toleration therefore means, not human inability to possess some part of truth, but rather that the unending contest between truth and error is deliberately transposed from the field of social or political summary decision to the field of rational persuasion. The free process is required because fallible human beings, seeking truth, have a *right to become sure of it through their own free discovery* as they could hardly become sure through a dictated rightness. Toleration, rightly understood, means respect for the unique process through which each individual corrects his own errors; there is a preciousness of the search for truth which cannot be replaced by a gift of the final result.

The underlying position is that the standards of truth are intrinsic. The truth of history or of science is to be judged by standards of evidence determined by the subject matter and freely open to all men. The political arm has no privileged access to these standards; they reduce all powers to their own democracy. If a state were to require a scientist to publish such science as it approved, or a historian to teach the divine genealogy of an emperor, the outrage would consist not in the disregard of the scholar's private wishes but in overriding the nature of evidence which prescribes its rules to both ruler and ruled. The same outrage would exist if the scholar were required on state compulsion to publish the precise truth. For any political intrusion renders suspect the integrity of the action of a standard imperiously exclusive in its command of the result and inherently free.

17. FREEDOM OF EXPRESSION IS NOT AN UNCONDITIONAL RIGHT

The right to be in error in the pursuit of truth does not include a moral right to be deliberately in error, rejecting the pursuit of truth. The assumption of toleration, that the tolerated error is an incident in a genuine effort for light, is in such a case unfounded.

As in our previous discussion of freedom in general,[9] the grounds given for a claim of right define the conditions under which alone the claim is valid. Since the claim to the rights of free speech and free press rests on duty of a man to his thought and to his social existence, when this duty is ignored or rejected—as it is rejected when the issuer is a liar, an editorial prostitute whose political judgments can be bought, a malicious inflamer of unjust hatred—the ground for his claim of right is abandoned.

This point is simple, inescapable, pivotal, and generally overlooked. We leave it with this bare statement and proceed to its consequences.

9. Above, p. 73.

18. LAPSE OF MORAL RIGHT DOES NOT OF ITSELF UNSEAT LEGAL RIGHT

If the ground of the claim of right is freely abandoned, the moral right lapses; the legal right may remain. This does not mean that the law is indifferent to the motives of the man who claims protection of the right of freedom of the press. But it does mean, among other things, that law is at a disadvantage in judging motives. It can offer no infallible test to distinguish between being in error inadvertently and being in error with intention to defraud. It has indeed frequently to judge motives and to assess good will and good faith, but it moves with reluctance into this invisible region.

Nor does it belong to the province of law to enforce morals, eliminating those departures from inner rightness which are part of the moral pilgrimage of the individual soul. Lying is itself an exercise of freedom, belonging—for the youthful adventurer in word-using and others—to the field of experimental morals. Speech is given to us, in the form of a voluntary activity subject to invisible control, in order that we may hide our thought if we so choose. Living in a lying world is thus part of the normal experience of man, and with it comes in due time a skill in detecting the liar. Where minds are actively meeting, the lie tends to react on the liar; still more so the habitual indulgence in misrepresentation and deceit. Where there are other sources of necessary information, the lying press tends to lose patronage as well as repute, though in present conditions it seldom loses enough to vanish. Thus, the press does to some extent correct the most substantial warpings of its own veracity and fairness when its colleagues are free either to tell the truth or to present their own partisan distortions in rebuttal. Whether or not these internal correctives, and the development of a sophisticated immunity to current types of falsehood, furnish a sufficient defense of individual and social interests is a question of fact. But in any case, if there could be an effective legal requirement that all men at all times should tell the truth and the whole truth, one great branch of moral self-discipline would disappear in an intolerable mechanical correctness. The freedom to lie is a condition of the moral value of telling the truth.

It is not the function of law to compel men to be moral, but at most to act as if they were moral.[10] The law is, however, obliged to assume the prevalence of the moral basis of its accorded rights. The legal right can operate as a principle of community structure only when this moral assumption is generally valid, and abuse is the exception. It moves with a known and accepted risk of affording cover to a minority who abuse freedom, in order to secure by its inelastic implements the invaluable privilege for the majority who deserve it. It will shield all users of speech and press, responsible and irresponsible, at least until some type of abuse of this liberty becomes a material injury to others and so far tangible that punitive or remedial action can be defined.

19. BUT THE LEGAL RIGHT ITSELF CANNOT BE UNCONDITIONAL

It follows from what has already been said that if there were in the community a wholesale abandonment of the moral basis of a legal freedom, that particular freedom

10. *The educational function of law should not, however, be overlooked.*—HUTCHINS.

would become unworkable; hence the legal right itself stands under this implied condition. But for individuals also the enjoyment of freedom of speech and of the press has its conditions; when the exercise of these freedoms takes the form of libel or slander, misbranding, obscenity, incitement to riot, sedition in case of clear and present national danger, law steps in with remedies, sometimes with suspensions. We have indicated these limitations in our previous chapter[11] and shall shortly inquire whether they have some common principle which it will be useful to formulate.

These limitations are for the most part of long standing in Anglo-American tradition. Their existence raises the question whether recent developments in the position and power of the press in contemporary society do not uncover further abuses calling for legal remedy.

That there are abuses which distinctly raise that question is beyond doubt. If our freedom claimer is a deliberate and persistent purveyor of adulterated news and purchased opinions, the inherent inaccessibility of mental states would not prevent cumulative evidence of intent. Whether in a particular case the state would be disposed to single him out from others and withdraw from him alone the shelter of its Bill of Rights, it would remain true that he deserves no such shelter and that all

11. *Above, pp. 73–75. As Zechariah Chafee points out, "constitutional freedom of the press is not regarded by the Supreme Court as an absolute right." And the Bills of Rights in all state constitutions, except those of Massachusetts, New Hampshire, Vermont, South Carolina, and West Virginia, in providing for the right to speak, write, and publish freely, explicitly add the condition "being responsible for the abuse of that right." See also Justice Frankfurter in the case earlier cited, Pennekamp v. State of Florida.*

the apologies for toleration falter in his case. No defense that has ever been given for free speech or press has intended to encourage the systematic spread of falsehood or the disguising of the actual aims of speech, as in concealed propaganda or the deceptive arts of the publicity expert so far as he is a purchasable promoter of any paying cause. Capitalizing the prejudices of human nature, inflaming latent hatreds, exaggerating the momentum of emotions already excessive, fanning suspicions, commercializing the potential vulgarities of the crowd— these practices, definable in the words we have used, identifiable in the facts, and visibly growing in skill and effect, are uses of freedom which have no relation to its tenable grounds. They may still elude our power of definition for the techniques of the courts, and most of them may be fitter for other than legal methods of correction. But the first step toward dealing with them is to recognize that the *ground upon which they could make a claim of right is gone;* they have forfeited it. If the law were to proceed against such practices, it would proceed against no moral claim.

20. PRESUMPTION AGAINST THE EXTENSION OF LEGAL REMEDIES TO CHECK OBVIOUS ABUSES

Reluctance to resort to legal remedies is not merely the prolongation of a traditional sentiment. Nor is it due primarily to the difference in social function between law and morals, above noted. Nor yet to the very substantial consideration that if freedom of expression is so important a right that our government secures it even against its own encroachment, any invitation to government to weaken this, its own barrier, must be an act of last resort.

All these influences co-operate to strengthen the presumption against defining new crimes or adding to existing censorships. But the main reasons are these: that the action of government in such cases is attended with special difficulties arising in part from its own nature[12] and in part from the nature of expression and that the process of free expression has some tendency to develop its own correctives.

Obviously, government will always be in a position to interfere with expression of opinion and make things difficult for a too ardent opponent. It will always have legitimate occasions for admonition or request; and these may shade into illegitimate occasions and motives: the political menace to freedom is a fundamental and continuing menace. If as a party in most public issues, government cannot be an unbiased arbiter or inquisitor of public debate, it becomes hazardous to invoke government freely for corrective action; every new definition of an abuse invites abuse of the definition. If the recognized instances for legitimate state action multiply, the facilities also multiply for concocting the appearance of abuse to justify a desired interference. Further, the tools of legal action—statutes, courts, juries, administrators— are not promising instruments for the nice discrimination of truth and falsehood and the other qualities of the output of expression. In proportion to the ease of political action, the possibilities of coercion hang over the process

12. These matters are dealt with in greater detail, as matters of law, in the full report by Zechariah Chafee, Jr., on *Government and Mass Communications,* published by the Commission.

of public debate and introduce an element of uneasiness into it, reducing its effective freedom beyond the range of actual encroachment, and troubling the accuracy of aim of the expression falling within its shadow. If government *may* pounce, many a speaker will give danger a wider berth than he ought to give.

The intrinsic objection to governmental action in the field of the citizen's expression is the logical ineptitude of presenting political thought as a result of the citizen's thought. For since it is only the *result* of the private thought-process which lends itself to control, not the process itself, whatever is altered by external pressure is no longer "expression." When and in so far as the goal of a thinking process is determined by an outside power, the process that leads to *that* goal is not thinking![13]

Consider, for example, the difficulties which would attend any effort to punish falsehood, involving at times a legal determination of what is true.

The absence of hard and fast lines between deliberate falsehood and the distortions due to partisan zeal which are part of the rough game of the democratic process make the steps of legal procedure hazardous. The same is true of the vagueness of line between fact and interpretation; lies in regard to matter of fact, in which evidence can most easily be brought, are frequently less important than *the color given to the fact*. Lies which consist in deliberate misreading of the *meaning* of facts, perhaps the most important lies, would be hardest to demonstrate in court.

Akin to the above, there is the ease of falsifying without lying, as by the omission of relevant facts. There is

13. See above, p. 108.

115

no more effective type of lie than a skilfully biased selection of truth. Legal action against lying would simply drive the wilful deceiver to the higher ingenuities of language. But the mere existence of legal sanctions against lying would be usable, and would most certainly be used, against the utterance of such truth as any determined body of citizens wished not to hear or not to allow to spread. Existing laws of libel are often tools of intimidation by unscrupulous partisans. Any extension of law penalizing abusive types of utterance would inevitably add to the dangers of telling any sort of unwelcome truth and would make more difficult the "courage of disclosure," possibly the most needed development in the use of free speech and free press. If a true story contains an incidental error, it is possible to fasten upon that error as a lie, and thus give a lying impression that the whole story is false, depriving the public of needed truth.

Because of this inherent ineptitude of legal remedies to deal with press abuses where they originate, namely, in the ingenious duplicities of the mind, the burden of proof will rest on any proposal for extending the scope of these remedies. The pertinent and direct cure for diseases of expression lies in the interchange of thought itself; in so far, therefore, as the inherent corrective factors within human intercourse have a reasonable likelihood of coping with the mischief, even needed and justified legal correctives must be held in abeyance.

That press lying has its own consequences to meet from the contemporary press and from its readers we have already noticed.[14] A large part of the disease car-

14. Above, p. 110.

ried by the stream of communication is shed by the freedom not to listen and by the more positive freedom to choose one's sources of comment. More is accounted for by a natural prophylaxis present in the human mind, especially if the natural dispositions to fair judgments are reinforced by early training. Modern life brings its own sophistications and develops a knowing sales resistance to the more usual varieties of deceit. Tough immunities can bear tough assaults, and there is a general presumption that a sound civilization develops and enjoys using an increasingly tough immunity.

21. LIMITS OF IMMUNITY FROM STATE INTERFERENCE

Whether in any case the inherent corrective factors of the processes of communication are adequate to meet the growing inventiveness of abuse, magnified in its scope by the increasing force of the instruments of communication, must remain a question of fact.

If in fact people in large numbers are being deceived, injured, or degraded by the manner in which others are using their freedom to speak or print or show pictures; if in fact numbers are being exploited or misled by Dowies or Fathers Divine, or are systematically entrapped by the protagonists of a current social infatuation, economic, political, or recreational, the public authority *cannot retreat behind the presumptive superiority of inaction.* There are abuses of speech and press which require political curb.

The state has, for example, no competence to pronounce upon religious truth, and for the sake of religious truth it must remain out of the discussion. But when a religious movement offends public order, morals, or sanity, the state must "by its fruits" judge it in error and limit freedom for the sake of freedom.[15] If the spontaneous defenses are not working, freedom is not served by pretending that they are.

If men are not in fact being made strong by developing resistance to current folly, banality, corruption of dignity, and solicitation to vice through the various agencies of the press, including the ingenious and perfumed pressures of a psychologically pointed, aesthetically distinguished, and morally dehydrated advertising onslaught, the plea for freedom on the ground that it provides a strong citizenship is proceeding on pleasing hypotheses contrary to fact, in the existing circumstances.

There is validity in the kindly assumption of political liberalism that mankind taken in the large is not only educable but desirous of being educated and that in this interest men will not only play a winning game against the progressive cleverness of deceit but gain skill in the process. Only, this stern will to unmask delusions is a variable; it is softened, especially in prosperous and secularized societies, by a tenderness toward delusions which flatter and indulge. In any society there is likely to be a limit at which, in point of fact, the educative process at the mass level ceases to advance, while skilled and interested fraud caters profitably to its increasing

15. *This remark seems to me to require careful qualification. See the decisions of the Supreme Court in regard to Jehovah's Witnesses.*—HUTCHINS.

—I agree that "public order" needs definition, remembering the time when Salvation Army street meetings were scored on this ground. But somewhere in this area there is a position to hold.—W. E. H.

groups of grateful addicts. This point appears to me to have been reached with the typical metropolitan public in this country. Since there is enjoyment in all passion, a man who hates will pay to have his hate increased, and a news sheet which feeds his flame will have his applause and his pence. Bigotry, lust, and prejudice follow similar laws. Find the rising wave of emotion, whatever it is, and so write as to exaggerate it; this is a good rule for financial advantage in all sections of the press. And when the cultivation of this rule is the prevailing phenomenon on the press landscape, it is useless to cite the maxim that humbug tends to educate the public. Liberalism is in the prisoner's dock at this moment of history, because it has lived on assumptions contrary to fact; it has taken the educability of mankind, which is real enough, as equivalent to the strong and persistent purpose of mankind to be educated, which is as a rule valid for only a few years after a process of liberation from bondage.

The purpose to gain wisdom through the chaos of impressions showered upon the public by the contemporary press involves a determination and a steering capacity which few maintain far beyond the direct logic of their own occupational and social interests; the pursuit of a socially uniting truth wilts and yields diminishing returns.

If at any time existing facts indicate that the case for freedom has thus reached a boundary, what has society to do? Here it is in order to revert to the question earlier raised: What is the principle of those legal limitations of free speech and press already recognized?

22. THE PRINCIPLE GOVERNING STATE INTERFERENCE

On the surface it appears that there is no one principle, unless compromise is a principle. There are a variety of policies at work, chiefly the following three: (i) that freedom does not include a privilege to injure tangible interests of other persons; (ii) that the right of freedom must yield to the interest of general security in cases of clear and present danger; and (iii) that as in statutes regarding obscenity the right of freedom may have to yield to the obligation of law to support the most vulnerable standards and ideals of the community.[16]

16. *If drawing the line to define proper governmental regulation of individual expression on grounds of obscenity is not to be a series of piecemeal adjustments, we need to define the line more sharply. The vague formula here which justifies public interference in support of "the standards and ideals of the community" provides no defense against suppression on behalf of whatever the current custodians of the mores of a majority determine is bad. Some of the recent judicial and administrative pronouncements (see Chafee,* Government and Mass Communications, *section on "Protection of the Common Standards of the Community") seem to be moving toward a definition which has a close affinity with the theory Hocking has established for individual expression generally in sections 10–17. There he builds a basis in moral right for the individual who has something to say and establishes it as a right the state should protect. He excludes from protection under that right the individual who engages in conscious deception, concealed propaganda, whose opinions are for hire, or who consciously "commercializes the potential vulgarities of the crowd." Applied to the field of obscenity, this would exclude all that we call "pornography," which has the purpose of stimulation of the sex impulse for financial gain. It would, however, protect against governmental intrusion honest expression of artistic and social conviction in matters of sex, as in other fields. It would not, of course, prevent limitations to special audiences (medical fraternity, adults) of written or other expressions addressed primarily to such audi-*

The common idea in these cases seems to be that of practical adjustment among conflicting obligations of law,[17] of which the obligation to individual liberty paramount

---

*ences. Whether in this field the legal rule will follow the definition of moral right is a doubtful possibility in the present climate of thinking and feeling regarding such matters. But the argument from principle for so doing would seem to be as compelling here on grounds of the basic individual right of utterance and the social value of criticism, as in the discussion of other institutions and ideas.—*LEIGH.

*—A distinction should be made in law and in fact between the business of the panderer, who exploits the random sex impulses of the public for his financial profit, and the actual publication of obscenity, in which the criterion is not the motive of gain but the actual content of the piece. This, I think, is a matter of great difficulty; and one trouble with the task of the censors, always a target for ridicule, is the fact that their definitions have been drawn perforce from intuition and not from official formulas. Not that official formulas would be more accurate and enlightening but that they would constitute for the censor a refuge and a defense. The fact that obscenity is at least half in the mind of the observer, rather than entirely in the thing observed, and is a factor of this purpose —as a medical chart might convey obscenity to a mind devoid of the professional purpose—adds to the difficulty. Nevertheless, with the aid of psychology, a definition of obscenity should be attempted as a part of our own undertaking. The sketch of such a definition will appear below (p. 122).—*W. E. H.

17. *This position is accepted, often with acknowledged regret, by certain high authorities in jurisprudence, Roscoe Pound, Radbruch, and others. Chafee at times seems to adopt it. Radbruch goes so far as to say that there is an irreconcilable conflict among the goals of law, especially between the goal of individual liberty and the goal of communal security. Pound's interpretation of the law of torts is governed by the antithesis between individual responsibility for acts of will and such legal phenomena as liability without fault in which the dominating motive is the social calculability of the incidence of injury.*

in the nineteenth century now begins to retire in favor of the general interest in security and order. Yet compromise and adjustment are assuredly tentative policies, uncomfortable not alone in theory but also in practice. Can a single principle for the legal limitation of freedom be found?

In each of the three types of legal limitation on free expression above mentioned, the free activity is affecting adversely an external interest. This implies that expression has become something else than the utterance of opinion: *It has moved out of the half-world between thought and action; it has become a deed.* A libel is not an expression of opinion, destined to stir a system of differing opinions; it is an attack, destined to bring down the stock of a fellow-man in the eyes of his neighbors and perhaps of his employer. A published obscenity is not an idle mental image: it is a disruptive mental image, a violent displacement of the self-sense of the viewer from the region of active purpose to the region of bodily preoccupation; it intrudes upon the eye what is normally in the province of touch and concealment; it begins a psychological disintegration. An inflammatory speech may be as much an act as a cry of fire. The immunities proper to public debate cannot be invoked to cover a mode of aggressive social action under the guise of the expression of thought. Whatever the state's responsibility may be toward the injured interests or rights, that responsibility must operate precisely as if the verbal expression were a physical attack.

The state must be sure that the boundary between expression and deed has been passed. The adverse effect on other interests must be *serious, overt, and demonstrable.*

122

Otherwise the notion of injury through expression becomes too wide a category, for no human utterance is totally devoid of physical effect; the state dare intrude on speech or press only when it is beyond doubt that it has a duty to intrude.

And in such cases the interest which we say the state must defend is an interest *also of the aggressor*. This is obvious in the case of a danger to public security. It is less so in the case of libel. But here, also, the libeler has no desire to lower the security of reputation-in-general; he would still assert his right to his own repute and hence that of all others except his particular victim. The interest injured or threatened by the aggressor is therefore *not wholly external* to him; in attaching a punitive sanction to his conduct, the law acts in his behalf also.[18]

If this analysis is correct, the action of the state is in none of these cases accurately described as a compromise or an adjustment between clashing interests. A's right of free speech does not yield *partially* to B's interest in his social standing; there is no moral or legal right to libel another person *a little*. When expression becomes libel, its right stops short.[19] The interference of the state

18. *This seems not to relate to the rebel who may have a real interest in treason, or may hope to find good fishing in dangerously troubled social waters, so that he wants social stability endangered. Or it seems to assume that the rebel accepts the idea of rights that are the same for all, as he is likely not to do. And the passage seems to refer to generic rights as wholes, rather than to marginal adjustments where compromise seems constantly to be involved. This aspect naturally occurs to an economist, brought up in the school that treated values as incremental.*—CLARK.

19. *Just as long as there are two genuine rights involved, the state is bound to protect both of them. Ordinarily there is no conflict. But an apparent conflict may emerge in either of two cases,*

moves into a vacated region of the "right of freedom of expression." It interferes, however, not *because* the moral right has been abandoned by the aggressor, but because in that vacancy of moral right there is a positive right of the victim and of society which has to be asserted in its full force and extent.

The case is somewhat different when aggressive expression affects public order or security rather than private rights. In suppressing inflammatory speech in cases of clear and present danger, there is no imputation of ill will or criminal intent upon the speaker. The moral right to speak may remain intact, and the liberty of the speaker appears to be simply overriden by a major interest. By common consent the public safety takes precedence over personal liberty. And the public action is not punitive but preventive; expression is, as far as possible, stopped at its source. Here the conflict between individual right and the common good is at its sharpest.

Nevertheless, here also the action of the state is not an external limitation on freedom, in the nature of a compromise. For the interest of the aggressive speaker is also on the side of the public security. Not only outwardly, but in his own mind, his right to free expression is subordinate to the central interest of the human will, that of *doing one's job in the world.* Unless there is a

---

when A maliciously lies about B, or when B's reputation is a sham, and A injures it by telling the truth. In the first case, the right of A is forfeited. In the second case, the apparent right of B vanishes. Speech is not subject to legal restraint merely because it hurts sombody; unless it were free to inflict all the pain involved in tearing down established and venerable frauds, it would be deprived of one of its most useful services.

stable course of human history, there is no job to do and no part to play. If he could believe the state right in judging that his free expression endangers the general order or security, he would be with the state; he also would curb his partial freedom for the sake of his total freedom.[20]

He cannot surrender the right of his own opinion as to whether the state's judgment is correct that the boat is being rocked, or whether it may need a bit of rocking in order to provide a better historical context for human action. The tragic possibility of a head-on clash of his ultimate moral right and the state's opinion is not excluded. The duty of the state to suppress the speaker may be as unquestionable as the duty of the speaker to resist being suppressed. But this is not the normal relation of the two wills; in the usual situation, if the state silences the speaker, it is his will to be silenced. For no one wants to speak unless there is a continuous human society to contain the effect of his words. His right to speak is relative to the condition of the historical order because it is his absolute right to have a place in history.

It follows that in all cases of the presently accepted legal restriction on free expression, we have something better than compromise: we have a principle. If we could venture to give that principle a formal expression, it might be this:

20. *Here Hocking is dealing with those legitimate and honorable attitudes, whose claim to freedom is unquestioned, partly because it could be trusted to accept necessary restraints. What is said here seems to have no application to the genuinely criminal mentality, or to treasonable activities by a patriotic enemy alien whose patriotism is not ours so that he deliberately wants our security endangered.*—CLARK.

When expression becomes equivalent to aggressive action, it incurs the general legal responsibilities of action. If it injures in a serious, overt, and demonstrable manner legitimate interests, or if it endangers public security and order, the state is not alone justified in acting; it ought to act, to remedy or prevent the injury. Such action is a limitation of liberty in the interest of the greater liberty both of the injured or endangered and of the aggressor himself.

This is the principle of existing limitations of free speech and press. If new categories of abuse were to come within this principle, the responsibilities of government would require their consideration with the question in mind whether specific punitive or preventive measures would do more harm than good. The burden of proof would rest upon any proposed extension of these categories of state action. But the general presumption against legal action is not intended to render society inert or helpless before possible new developments of misuse of the immense powers of the contemporary press.

The principle we have stated would exclude state action in the great majority of cases in which, while the ground of right is abandoned, the error is primarily moral; lying speech would for the most part be rejected as a ground of legal action. It would admit as proper areas of legal action certain types of abuse not yet touched by law. False propaganda or outrageously false report, especially in regard to international situations affecting peace, might be so far overt, demonstrable, and pernicious as to demand and admit legal remedy.[21] And while it is the task of a treatise on principle to indicate the criteria which mark the type of abuse for which legal remedy is fitting, rather than to propose what cases meet those criteria, I may offer my own impression that complete legal passivity toward the "liberty to degrade" and toward the growing vices of the publicity racket is, in the existing condition of our public mind, ceasing to be a virtue of this free state. Explicit extensions of the definitions of fraud and bribery to bring the purchase of editorial opinion clearly within their scope ought in my view to be considered.

As to the possible nature of such a remedy, it would be an obvious maxim that the light touch of government is generally preferable to severe or exemplary actions; a law requiring retraction, for example, would be preferable to a law suspending a publication. This problem is discussed in detail in the Chafee report (*Government and Mass Communications*).

Something more may be learned—by likeness and by contrast—from the free conspiracy of scientific labor and publication to a common advance. Science is, in a sense, the special and prize instance of freedom of thought and expression (remember that the spectacle of Galileo in his old age, in durance in Italy, helped to stir young Milton to make England a fairer place for such men). Science is man at the face of the mine, it is man attacking the unknown; his yield is surprise for himself and others—it is the stuff that news is made of. In its nature scientific research must be free from all dictation, and its results not what the scientist nor any authority but what

21. See above, pp. 35–36.

nature—as reported on the honor of the observer—makes them. Yet science has its rules of procedure, which are essential to the value of its results. Not every tyro can come in and play with the cyclotron. Not every crank who wants to waste his time on devising perpetual motion can get his articles into the scientific journals. Science is today a firm fraternity, selecting its own continued membership. There is a strict gateway of access to the great instruments, the livings, the grants, the preferments, the publications. There is a powerful though unwritten orthodoxy, based on the idea that science is a whole and that individual efforts must be competently co-ordinated to effect its organic growth. There is always a fringe of dubious subjects, like psychical research and certain aspects of psychology, looked at askance by the scientific Center, the church universal of Physics. The trouble with psychology from the scientific point of view is that everybody can and does work at it with or without qualifications, because he carries around with him, in his own self-awareness, the most necessary part of the laboratory; and, with this, he can probably get his stuff into the papers, to the horror of scientific psychology. The god of science is already a jealous god and rejects the worship not alone of the quack, of the commercial exploiter of discovery, the slipshod and the incompetent, but also, and with the firmest hand, of anyone who manipulates or falsifies his evidence. The work of the general press is in many ways the exact opposite of the work of science: it must be swift, unfinished, impressionistic; it could accept with difficulty any orthodoxy even of method; its personnel must have a freer range. But it may take from the picture of scientific advance this principle: that the utmost freedom is not alone consistent with, but requires, a recognized set of standards for one's work, and a feeling for the necessary reference of every man's work to that of every other in building for the public a coherent picture both of the day's events and of the day's debate. It is this *coherence and reliableness* with which the community is chiefly concerned; and while the hand of the state is as disturbing in the press as it is in the work of science—it might initiate and aid efforts to explore the possibilities of a self-administered set of standards.

This is but one phase of the confusion which results from interpreting freedom as an implied invitation to unlimited private emission of the signs of thought without regard to the pattern which the total output makes on the minds of potential consumers. The state cannot rightly intervene in this "democratic process" to control its result. This does not forbid an attempt on its part to reduce the chaotic character of the process itself to a degree of coherence and rationality. Those who prescribe or alter the rules of a game in the interest of fairer play are not dictating who shall win; they are promoting the freedom of players and observers alike. The same is true of the position of society vis-à-vis public discussion.

The institution of the ballot is the most conspicuous example of community action in this interest. The essence of the ballot is the predated decision on a specified issue or issues;[22] it is an act closing a debate. The announcement of a future ballot brings at once a (limited) structure and purpose into the relatively formless churning of the public mind over an indefinite plurality

22. See above, p. 94.

of issues, which the magazines of opinion struggle to shape and tend to multiply. In its nature it cannot go beyond the narrow range of decisions which the public is authorized to make. This range is extended by more or less systematic straw ballots now in much vogue; but since they represent no genuine public act, and ignore debate as a necessary preliminary to responsible opinion as distinguished from casual impression, they can do little to focus public thought. Their prevalence indicates, however, a widely felt need of treating public debate at least as seriously as the public treats a game, and suggests a method of advance.

23. PUBLIC RESPONSIBILITY FOR THE PROCESS OF PUBLIC DEBATE

We have commented on the failure of the present unregulated and profuse output of expression to conspire to any common meaning or result. In a sense, this is as natural a consequence of free expression (stimulated or not by financial rewards) as the growth of jungle is natural in the tropics—especially in a society not given to taciturnity. There are societies instinctively noisier per capita than ours; but no others have as yet the mechanical ability to extend the range and force of individual utterance so greatly. This overproduction—shall we say of thought?—tends to defeat itself by eliciting in its intended audience a high-grade psychological deafness through which only a small percentage of the bombardment penetrates. And that small part is selected from within in such wise as to render more or less futile the psychological arts of "publicity" which promise irresistible domination of attention. If they could deliver what they promise, they would reduce their victims to will-less automata. Their attention-assaulting performance masquerading as freedom of speech or press is as antisocial as it is ridiculous; we submit to this scientifically outfitted emotional brigandage only because we see no good way to fend it off. Our feebleness of political invention contrasts sadly with the fertility of the attack.[23]

We may thus state as a second principle of the public touch on free speech and press: *The state may act to supervise or regulate the intermingling of the free products of expression so that what is true and valuable in these products may have a fighting chance with the kind of public actually present.*[24]

This principle as stated assumes that expression itself remains unlimited. "Overproduction of expression" is a phrase whose meaning lies not so much in the objective phenomenon of profusion as in the limited capacity of consumers to find their own way through the wilderness. For this embarrassment there are now various

23. *Though we might learn something from our own success in curbing the "free speech" of street hawkers or the competitive din of porters and drivers at stations and seaports as seen in the contrast between scenes of debarkation at Alexandria and Southampton. We are making a beginning by way of local ordinances regarding blatant and offensive advertising, billboards destroying the character of highways, and other intrusions on landscapes, seascapes, airscapes, in the interest of fraudulent egotisms. But these touch only slightly and negatively the edges of the immense problem of bringing together rationally the expresser and the needers of expression. It requires affirmative as well as negative handling, as in the municipal provision of public auditoriums, whose administration, freed from party interests, might canalize and select what the public is invited to see or hear.*

24. See above, pp. 92–95, 129.

private enterprises offering guidance to those who despair of guiding themselves: vicarious reading and vicarious selection become gainful specialties for minds that can ingest, digest, and judge prodigiously for the nondistinctive average man. The community has concern with this process at several points, such as the new type of authority which substitutes itself for individual choice, and the tendency to make facility rather than depth the mental quality most useful for survival. But the *state* is concerned with its effect on the presentation of public issues and on the unity of the nation. Confusion is incompatible with the existence of public opinion; distraction and incompetent criticism are incompatible with public unity; both are incompatible with democracy.

It is here that we have seen the widest defection in Europe from the liberal view of a free press. The Soviet system rejects diversity as having any virtue at all in respect to the ideology and the main business of state (see pp. 27–28 above). Wherever the working unity of the state is founded on will, rather than on reason and open discussion, the same attitude will be found; it is a necessary consequence of denying the existence of common standards of truth and value. It is also a consequence of conceiving the state primarily in terms of action.

As long as the state is considered as caring chiefly for public order and its own existence, its unity is not affected by free internal discussion; consent to the existence of the state, human nature being what it is, remains necessarily unanimous. In proportion as the state engages in active enterprise, long-range policies, programs, planning, etc., diversity of opinion has a different impact. Divergent thoughts become divergent deeds.

British experience, firm to the last ditch on freedom of expression, finds that public planning puts a new light on the "right to criticise"; "no long-time plan can succeed if you go chipping away at it every five minutes." The distinction we need is that *between a fundamental belief and a working hypothesis.* The fundamental belief you must always be able to debate. The working hypothesis is more fragile, more subject to ruin by dissent; it therefore demands, for its own duration, a greater conformity. The time for questioning is before and after the experiment, not while it is on—otherwise there is no experiment. This, the dictate of good sportsmanship, is also the dictate of good politics.

The totalitarian states have failed to make this distinction. Conceiving the state solely in terms of will, and seeing this will committed to a public program calling for unanimity of effort, they call also for unanimity of belief. At most, the state can call for unity in working hypothesis. It is precisely the ideology, the ultimate belief, that must remain open to debate, if the unity of the state is to be a living reality rather than an imposed convention. Marx has misled his followers by a false antithesis: "Philosophy has been a reflection on the world, whereas the task is to change it." The task is always to change the world, but to what end? A free reflection on the ends of change must be a working partner in all change that is intelligent rather than blind.

24. THE DUTY OF A FREE SOCIETY TO MAINTAIN ITS OWN PRINCIPLES

A free society cannot be indifferent to the promulgation of doctrines which threaten the very liberties claimed by those advocates. The contemporary world is familiar with the activities of movements which utilize free institutions to undermine free institutions. The self-contradictory nature of such activity must be one of the clear intuitions of men who care for the preservation of liberty. The principle of freedom is bound to believe in itself and to act positively to maintain its political existence.

Nevertheless, it is as a rule equally bound not to act in a reverse self-contradiction by suppressing liberty in order to preserve liberty.

Criticisms of democracy, and of the rights of free men, must be entertained by a democracy, not silenced as if in fear that a rational defense must be ineffective. The criticisms are to be entertained as tolerated errors, which, if we have understood our own work, we can meet on their own ground. But they are also to be entertained as helpful half-truths, until such time as our democracy has no faults which honest or half-honest criticism can help to remedy. If our democracy had been above criticism, its enemies would have been less formidable.

There is a point at which tolerance must cease. That is when (as the fate of President Ebert in republican Germany may illustrate) the strict use of democratic methods among men not fully aware of their meaning tends to throw power into the hands of the enemies of the democratic state. It is one of the intrinsic evils of history that an imperfect democracy may have to insist by force on the rights of its possible future as against the nonrights of its indefensible present.

4

NONPOLITICAL IMPEDIMENTS TO
PRESS FREEDOM

IN A normal modern state there is only one literally coercive power over adults—government. But government, as we have already observed (sec. 14 above), is neither the only, nor the original, nor the most prevalent menace to free expression. And, in proportion as the needful restraints on governmental interference are established in law and custom, the dangers from other sources become conspicuous. We are aware today that the most numerous and active impairments of freedom come from within society itself and that some of them require examination with the question of principle in mind. We shall consider three of them: (i) direct social pressures; (ii) effects of the character of the press as large-scale industry; and (iii) limitations of freedom from restricted access to truth and fact.

25. DIRECT SOCIAL PRESSURES

We must distinguish between pressure on opinion and pressure on the expression of opinion. Pressure on opinion is pervasive and inescapable; it constitutes no limitation of freedom; it is part of the atmosphere of a society living by ideas and by the propagation of those ideas to all comers; it is the aggressive part of social heredity. In so far as a society is individualist, it will silently promote individualism; in so far as it is collectivist, it will silently promote collectivism; by a hundred influences of suggestion, rather than by direct argument, it induces association with its view. Every type of society continues itself by these thought-saving pressures until it is deliberately challenged; and as long as challenge is possible, at which point "pressure" gives way to argument, no loss of freedom is involved.

Pressure on opinion can never be of a strenuous nature, since men's minds are not changed by strong measures; but pressure on the expression of opinion may run through a wide gamut of degrees. Wholly within the limits of law, it may mount until, through the incidental capacity of the pressure-using interest or institution to inflict social harm or to hold out painfully attractive inducements for conformity, it approaches coercion. Still, we must observe, as long as coercion is not actual, legal freedom remains intact; in a literal sense, expression is free whenever and wherever a man can say and print what he ought[1] to say and print and *take the natural consequences*. His freedom does not require that there be no consequences or that they shall be to his liking.

It is not even to the interest of speech and press, not to speak of their right, that they should escape the swarm of resolute and aggressive influences emanating from the environment of vested beliefs of a living society. That activity constitutes a test of the vigor of his thought which any new head aspiring to address the public ought to encounter. It is a relic of the faintly unreal sentiment

1. *"Ought"* or *"wants"*?—HUTCHINS.
—*"Sees fit."*—W. E. H.

with which the topic of toleration has been clothed if we picture our "independent thinker" as a man wholly sure of his own judgment in advance of any clash with those who differ. What the independent thinker wants is freedom not from opposition but from coercion; and this he has if the state, keeping its own hands off, sees to it that *none of these other pressures rise to the coercive point*—whether from current prejudices operating through the subscription list, or from advertisers, or from sources of investment capital, or from labor organizations, or from the dictates of institutionalized ideologies. If he is prepared to endure ostracism or to stand a boycott, he has still a literal freedom to say his say. It is not the function of the state to protect any utterer of ideas from the type of pressure we may call moral, nor would it be desirable that it should.

But the notion of "pressure" is ambiguous. Beside the pressures which are inseparable from the fact that men believe what they believe and oppose what they disbelieve, there are malign and corrupt pressures. Freedom of expression must include the freedom of unwelcome response to unwelcome speech; but must this response include a right to ostracize or to boycott or to buy off? What we have to do is to make a clear distinction of principle between legitimate and illegitimate social pressures and reactions.

Can the line be drawn between the *kinds of penalty*[2] which can be attached to obnoxious expression, perhaps as we have suggested between *relevant and irrelevant penalties?* If A dissents from B's views, and persists in his dissent in spite of B's efforts of persuasion, the im-

2. See above, p. 100.

mediately relevant penalty is B's mental disapproval; and if the subject matter involves a plan of action, then also an inability on B's part to invite or accept A's co-operation. Since the ideas over which men earnestly differ involve modes of behavior, the relevant penalty for dissent would be simply carrying into action the logic of disagreement. If a man reasons against a form of faith, he can hardly complain if he is excommunicated. One who like Spinoza had become inwardly heretical no longer *belonged* to the synagogue; to be excluded from it was a relevant and indeed a necessary hardship. Of the further penalties which in that day attached to excommunication, being forbidden to teach theology was certainly relevant; to be forbidden to teach anything, doubtfully relevant; to be deprived of a living by being cut off from ordinary intercourse with the congregation bordered on the excessive and irrelevant. Similarly, an attempt to secure conformity of expression by offering rewards requires the same distinction. If the reward of agreement is an opportunity of partnership, it is presumably a necessity of the situation, a relevant advantage; a cash bonus for agreement is irrelevant—the irrelevance defines the "bribe." On this ground we may say that freedom of speech and press, in respect to social presures, means *freedom from irrelevant penalties and inducements.*

The root of the trouble in corrupt social pressures is in the impulse to reward or punish expression. To punish means to add *extra* sufferings to those which the natural course of things entails; to reward means to add *extra* benefits. Reward and punishment, as going beyond what the consistency of action with thought requires, have no legitimate place whatever in the social response to the expression of thought. Expression that moves under the fear of deliberate penalty or in the hope of deliberate reward is to that extent unfree.

And since human beings, even in societies politically free, are more or less inclined to purchase agreement and penalize dissent, a normal social freedom of speech and press is still to be won. An appeal, like that of Mill, to the liberal spirit of the community is still timely,[3] and also an appeal to the integrity of the processes of persuasion. Are any other measures available or called for?

In the letter of the Bill of Rights, the press is protected from no constraints except those of legislation. There is no clear legal remedy for putting deliberate financial pressure on an editor who speaks an independent piece. It would seem reasonable to argue, however, that if freedom of the press is so significant that government will secure it against its own dispositions to encroach, it would be inclined to protect it, not alone against physical violence, but also against well-definable infringement from other quarters. A recent Supreme Court decision implies this view of the scope of our fundamental law—though in the cautious and negative language of a lawyer conscious of breaking new ground.[4] Protection from illegitimate pressures is a legitimate concern of

3. *"What I contend is that the inconveniences which are strictly inseparable from the unfavourable judgment of others are the only ones to which a person should ever be subjected for that portion of his conduct which . . . . does not affect the interest of others in their relations with him"* (On Liberty, chap. iv).

4. *Justice Black in U.S. v.* Associated Press (*326 U.S. 20*) held that *"freedom of the press from governmental interference under the First Amendment does not sanction repression of that freedom by private interests. . . . . Surely a command that the government itself shall not impede the free flow of ideas does not afford non-governmental combinations a refuge if they impose restraints upon that constitutionally guaranteed freedom."*

the law. Without attempting the impossible and pernicious enterprise of making social intolerance a crime, it would in my personal judgment be desirable to recognize for what they are the actually criminal extensions of pressure on speech and press, both in the direction of purchased expression, under the laws of bribery, and in the direction of intimidation or suppression.

For the legal approach, it is worth noting that illegitimate pressures on press utterances are not usually avowed, so that the utterance is not what it purports to be. Under the guise of an editorial opinion or a broadcast, the press may be voicing the thought of an owner, or the interest of an advertiser (with or without thought), or the demand of a coterie of financial backers or subscribers; in such cases the product is falsified as to its source. These same sources of pressure have their own right of free speech; they could come forward in their own name. But it is no part of their freedom, nor of any man's freedom, to control the voice of another, or to gain under any consideration the authority of another's mind. Wherever any group or interest invades, hampers, or warps the expression of any press medium, the absence of avowal should give ground for an action for fraud.

In such an action it is evident that the press will not complain of the invasion of its liberty, for it has become a party to the fraud; the corrupted is guilty with the corrupter. It is the public which is deceived and defrauded. The rights of the public in the integrity of press expression will play an increasing part in the future notion of a free press. There can be no press freedom to falsify the authorship of speech.

Since the subscribers must be free not to subscribe,

and supporters not to support, certain financial pressures upon unwelcome opinions are a normal part of the operation of social judgment. There can be no social presumption that morally courageous newssheets must survive, even if they are also mentally competent. Public irritability, stupidity, and intolerance have cost society many an important idea and will continue to do so until the social principle "no irrelevant penalties" has become a habit. The survival of an independent press in a highly opinionated and impatient society follows no law different from that of any individual commentator: if his judgment commends itself to the public in three points, he may buck the current in the fourth without being rejected; but the public will not allow him to oppose it on all points at once, nor yet to confine himself to a single point, however valuable, on which he exclusively harps. If he disobeys these precepts of pedagogy, the public will slay him, no matter what his merits; both will be the losers, and there is no actionable offense on either side. It is only when financial pressure has the deliberate aim of compelling a speaker or editor to conform in his views *while continuing to speak* that crime occurs. When speaker or editor yields to that pressure, there is a double crime which journalism should join with law and the moral sense of the public to make disreputable.

26. EFFECTS OF THE CHARACTER OF THE PRESS AS LARGE-SCALE ENTERPRISE

The dangers we have been speaking of relate to conscious pressures from outside the press. The danger now to be mentioned is from within the press structure itself and may not be conscious. Bias is a mental constraint which everybody is subject to and of which most are unaware, or but partly aware. Like the rest of mankind, editors are presumably biased, by personal experience and training, also by their professional habits. But there are special biases to which a large part of the contemporary press is liable because of its character (i) as a commercial enterprise whose terms of success are set by the business management, in view of the existing economy and the state of the public mind; (ii) as a large-scale enterprise interlocking both in finance and in personnel with the big industry of the nation; (iii) as an owner's enterprise in which much editorial ability is retained in the hire-and-fire relation of dependence; and (iv) as a competitive enterprise which through its growth and concentration tends to squeeze out of the productive picture many potential contributors of lesser stature or divergent trend.

It would be strange if these striking characteristics had no influence on the type of man reaching positions of control in the press today. The concentration of financial power, the seductive influence of control, the inevitable involvement of the press mind in the power-plant if not the engine-room of a technological era, the struggle for dominance between the business objectives and the content, might well engender attitudes similar to those of the industrial executive. Not that these attitudes are evil but that they are partial; whereas a business dealing in ideas, and addressed to the whole people, tacitly pretends to speak *for* the whole people and from a standpoint of "objectivity" transcending that of any special position or group interest.

It is a point of logical interest to note in what sense

freedom of the press may be said to be in danger from this source. Editors, speakers, authors, commentators, may be in full enjoyment of their freedom to publish what they want to publish; the bias, if there is one, affects only the sort of thing they want to publish. A bias is a mental bondage, but it is a bondage of which the victim makes no complaint! It is, nonetheless, a bondage, assuming that the person bound wishes a more objective view of truth; and it may be all the more serious for him and for the community that this bondage is so fully consistent with a pleasant psychological sense of perfect liberty.

How serious and widespread this kind of warping may be at any time is a question of fact, not of principle. Its existence is not open to doubt. If the work of the press were mechanical, the effect of bias might be ignored. But since this work is, in a sense, a daily work of swift art, in which every story requires pruning and proportioning, it will everywhere bear the imprint of the producer's trait. And since the industry as a rule accepts as a natural prerogative of ownership the control of editorial policy by owners, the question of whether they have an identifiable group-bent becomes a major issue of community freedom.

In regard to that bent, one prevalent superstition may be set aside, that of the "economic determination of opinion."[5] It is not true that a man's thinking is determined either by the source of his bread and butter, by

5. *The theory that economic groups are, by a fatality they know nothing about, doomed to think as they do has spread far beyond the Marx-Engels circles in which it originated. It still lies at the basis of the a priori Soviet judgments on American press freedom, which we noticed in our opening chapter (p. 36).*

his economic functions, or by his financial-group neighbors. His opinions do indeed grow, in part, out of his personal struggle for livelihood and success; but they have two roots—not one only—his experience and his reason. Through his reason he continually frees himself from the biases of his experience. His experience is linear —he can live along only a single life-line; but he can *think* the life-lines of all his contemporaries—he builds himself a whole picture which corrects the narrow slant of his experience. The occupation of journalism is about the worst possible for cherishing biases by maintaining innocence regarding other aspects of any social situation. If any newsman has a bias, he is daily accused of it; and a bias faced is no longer a bias but a more or less rationalized position. If, then, an editor remains mentally in chains, it is not because of any unconscious bias—it is his free choice and his bad conscience. There is no "economic determination" of press opinion; and, as any eye can see, there is no such fatal uniformity or group-mindedness among press owners as the theory of economic determination would require.[6]

6. *These statements seem to need qualification, but perhaps the discussion that follows supplies it sufficiently. An economist of my acquaintance, much in contact with pressure groups, claimed that he had encountered nothing else than group interest and even denied the existence of a "social point of view." Cf. p. 102, first whole paragraph.*—CLARK.

—Our method of self-government by competitive pressures on legislative bodies is indeed developing throughout the community a pressure-group ethic as a counterfeit substitute for democracy, together with a fool's-paradise feeling that the "social point of view" will take care of itself. How far is the press involved in this ethical shift?

I am very far from acquitting the press of participating in this

144

But the bent is there, and its psychological roots concern us. They are nothing more recondite, I think—apart from an unthinking susceptibility to prevailing social winds—than the commercialism of commerce and the interestedness of interest. In the course of its technical and financial development the press has become something that at first it was not, an active factor in the industrial system of the nation, and thus a directly interested party in the well-being of that system. And the maxim of wordly wisdom applies to it, when looked at statistically, that the *public cannot rely on any interested group for disinterested truth.* In other cases, it does not expect to do so; when a lawyer becomes judge, he ceases to act as counsel for interests which may come before his bench. But the press is ex officio judge of the

---

current corruption. What I am saying is that, where it does so, it is not through any subconscious economic necessity but with its eyes open. Thomas Hart Benton's statement, the statement of an artist, is more nearly accurate than the economic-determinism statement. He says:
"In a counting house society, newspapers must necessarily be influenced by counting house ideals. This will be so as long as counting house ideals remain socially dominant. No individual can permanently maintain superiority to his environment and be a successful part of it. Neither can a newspaper" (St. Louis Post-Dispatch Symposium on Freedom of the Press, 1938, *p. 14*).
I accept the phrase "influenced by"; I deny the "neither can." I say that, so far as the American press is "edited from the counting house," it is far more guilty than the conscience-dumb average of American business, because it is precisely the job of the press, while being in the scene, also to survey it; it is its duty to be self-conscious and to see the farce which the pressure ethic is making of democracy. My own observation is that on this point there is a wide variety in the press; there is nothing like a mechanical clique voice. Here and there I detect the glimmer of a "social point of view."—W. E. H.

145

system in which it is enmeshed; it is inescapably enmeshed in the system which it is bound to judge. One of the main reasons for calling on government to keep hands off the press is that government is an interested party in issues which the press must be free to discuss on all sides. What, then, if *the press* is an interested party in issues which the press ought to be free to discuss on all sides?

It is clear that the press is itself in a sort of dilemma; it can cease neither to be big business nor to judge big business. From this point of view, the stock complaint that the American press voices a dominantly "capitalistic" outlook is less a criticism than a truism. It would be a criticism only (i) if the *parti pris* of the majority press rendered it incapable of seeing and fairly reporting other types of social order and of recognizing defects in its own or (ii) if its defense of its own position were meretricious, composed of hollow plausibilities and half-truths. These twin vices, where they exist, are the real destroyers of confidence.

As a believer in freedom of the intellect, I assert that these vices need not exist either in our own or in any other system of economy. The principle that "no man can be a judge in his own case," useful as a prudential maxim, is psychologically inaccurate. Everyone does and should judge his own case, even when for social reasons he is also submitting it to an umpire or judge. The quality we call "justice," the capacity to see one's own case "objectively," i.e., with the eyes of the impartial observer, is one of the powers which makes man a human being. Journalists are not excluded either from this capacity or from the priesthood of administering

146

justice: their position as witnesses, together with their experience, should make them excel in it; they frequently rise to it—and that is enough to establish the possibility. It is also true that they frequently fail. There is a statistical likelihood that the incidence of ownership has much to do with these failures and that the recent decision of the British government after parliamentary debate to appoint a Royal Commission to conduct an inquiry into the ownership of British newspapers is a fair reminder of probable sources of prejudice. Something has to be attributed, also, to the social relation between a newspaper policy and its clientele; having issued a call to a certain segment of the public, a newssheet finds fresh personal analyses and deviations *from itself* increasingly difficult. Editorial judgment becomes the sustaining of a "position"—propaganda. And our system of freedom, helpless against most forms of press lying, is still more helpless against this close neighbor of the lie, partisan propaganda.

In American press discussions of economic issues the outright lie plays a less important role than the deficit of whole truth and the dissembling of issues. The prudent reader will not expect to gather the true inwardness of such a struggle as the recent coal strike from the official public statements, the oratory of Mr. Lewis, the backgrounded reports in the great dailies, or the heavy slugging of the labor press. He will sample two or more of these, and then perhaps seek some individual interpreter able to make sense of the mutually repellent fragments; for integrity is more frequently a quality of individuals than of groups. Thus in the late General Motors strike, Elinore Herrick made a notably enlightening statement in the *Herald Tribune* of December 3, 1945. The weeklies have a better chance than the dailies to present a well-interpreted picture; some of them do pretty well at it. But it is hard for any owner to stay out of all the ruts all the time. Even liberalism as a journalistic line committed to the overcom-

147

ing of all bias, and making a good fist of it to start with, too frequently becomes a victim of its own party and ends with a bitter orthodoxy of its own.

The total fact which the reader encounters is that he lives in a press world in which slanted and partisan utterance mingles with just judgment in uncertain proportions. There are good eggs in the omelette, but he is at a loss to identify them. And the moment of history in which he stands is one in which just judgment of social and economic issues is peculiarly momentous. Most of these issues hinge precisely on the problem how to administer the immensely increased power which an advancing technology is placing in human hands, individual or collective. The problem is unsolved. Its solution will not be promoted by the sole testimony of successful groups who, because they are successful, are not stung to explore the problem in its full extent. They lack the necessary nerves of pain. The press represents the sensory nerves of a nation, of a civilization; and if those nerves fail to dip into the areas of friction, failure, and suffering, their report must be wrong at one crucial point.

The public cannot expect to find "the truth" furnished it ready made by any speaker or writer; with the best efforts of the press, the reader must still work for it. But if the reader is constantly baffled, he may reach the conclusion that, for him, truth is not to be had, either because the "best efforts" of the press are not bent to that end, or because truth is inaccessible, or because it is "relative" and each interpreter has a right to his own. In the words of a French observer to one trying to get "the facts" about the operation of the Syrian mandate: "Ici, il n'y a pas des faits; il n'y a que des versions!" If

the typical American reader reaches this stage of disillusion, government by public opinion necessarily loses
its case and gives way to what we increasingly have, government by competing pressures, each of which has its
version "legitimately" corrupted by its interest.

The cure of the disease of bias does not lie in this
systematic surrender to its necessity.[7] It lies partly in a
new task of education, teaching Americans to read. Our
schools have been able to teach our people to read words
and sentences; they have not yet begun the task of teaching us to read truth out of miscellaneous part-truths,
which is the actual task of intelligent reading in our day.
It is an art with a technique and a morale of its own; it
is at least as important as the art of swimming, with

7. *Artist Thomas Hart Benton, whom we have quoted before,
notes the very close kinship between distortions of report due to
interest, and the distortion inseparable from all interpretative art:*
"*Newspapers have never been 'edited' in the interests of the
general public, which are too disguised to be precisely known,
but in the immediate graspable interests of political and economic
groups either having power and influence to keep or anxious to
attain these. Freedom of the press is the 'license' of the press to
represent facts so that the group of which it is a part may seem to
think and act on the side of Truth, Justice and God. Distortion by
suppression and emphasis is basic to editorial technique. . . . . As
this evil is, however, a greater or less condition of all expression,
nothing can be done about it*" (St. Louis Post-Dispatch Symposium on Freedom of the Press, 1938, *p. 14*).
*Compare with this the clear repudiation of "objectivity" as a
standard by the Soviet journalist Kuzmichev earlier quoted:*
"*All dissertations on 'objective and complete' information are
liberal hypocrisy,*" etc. (*p. 37 above*).
The fallacy here is that the conscious *attempt to move men by
distorted truth, as opposed to unconscious bias, fails to move
them, once they discover what the mover is doing; the only truth
that will continue to work is the truth that seeks objectivity, though
it fails to achieve it.*

149

which it has some kinship. Perhaps we should have called it the art of thinking while one reads.

But the burden cannot be placed even primarily on the reader. He has a moral right to consider the press, not an obstacle, but a first aid in his search for just judgment. And since in our system of liberty a free press must be legally free to distort, twist, omit, and lie up to a certain point, the cure will have to depend on an element of press honor. The dilemma of the large-scale-enterprise press which we have pointed out cannot be escaped; it cannot help being judge in its own case. It can help being the *sole* judge and the sole selector of witnesses. If a man becomes a trustee, it is customary for him to give a bond counterbalancing his conceivable interest in the yield of the trust; his giving of the bond involves no impeachment of his honesty of purpose. The work of the press is, in a sense, a public trust; the bond which it may freely offer is its willingness to summon witnesses from the opposition and from the neutral areas. This practice, already existing to some extent, will add much, as it is perfected, to the flagging public confidence in press performance. Even more important than the summoning of outside witnesses is the personal search for a justice of judgment, not unattainable, in which the diverging voices have already been heard; such a search speaks with a different voice from that of easy and raucous partisanship and wins in time its due authority.

From another quarter there are incidents of great organization, which, bringing many thinkers into a single hierarchy, tend to muffle the independent voices of the individual members. While the total number of persons engaged in mass communication has steadily increased, the over-all picture of the American press today shows a tendency to the assembling of these many minds into relatively few immense organizations. Each such pyramid of heads has, and must have as defining its personal identity, a more or less unitary editorial policy; the organization is, as a rule, the product of an ambition not primarily financial, the ambition to spread his own type of mind and outlook which makes the entrepreneur in the field of journalism. That he requires a vast assemblage of human ability to achieve this goal should not make it impossible of accomplishment; the pyramid has, let us say, a moral right to an identifiable policy. Yet its existence implies the subordination of many individual views to the corporate view, with a certain loss of their freedom of expression and a speculative net loss to the community in the "free flow of ideas."

There are two factors which mitigate this impression of stifled freedom: the relation of the individual to the organization is voluntary, and not every unit aspires to divergent expression. The existence of the organization provides for each member a career not otherwise available; the prestige of the total achievement accrues to each member; his opinion and attitude enter impersonally into the resultant editorial expression—the impact of his thought is not external, but it is not ineffective. Nevertheless, his thought remains anonymous, and his freedom to drop out of a corporation in which he has begun to build his career is less than perfect. He has an obligation of loyalty, an interest in his status, and a duty to his contractual commitments which sometimes may clash violently with his duty to his idea.

Since this situation, which may be relieved by an internal element of democracy and consultation within the organization, can never be perfectly cured; since it is inherent in the simple arithmetic of substituting, before the public, a single policy for a multitude of individual policies, the principle of individual freedom of expression acting alone would logically dissolve all such organizations by making clear the turpitude of an independent thinker who deliberately accepts their employment. This dilemma is to a certain extent a matter of theory rather than of practice. The intelligent pyramid bends to allow the expression of an able and valued worker, if only in a divergent footnote. If the divergence is occasional, it can be provided for; if it is persistent and constitutional, the worker clearly belongs elsewhere, or perhaps on his own, and the pyramid eases his transition. But the decisive consideration is (i) that, while the pyramid may make individual expression costly in terms of sacrifice, it can never make it impossible—freedom of speech is still literally intact; and (ii) society would almost certainly lose rather than gain if the pyramids were dissolved into the swarm of their individual speakers. The question is not solely one of the personal rights of utterance; it is also one of the rights of the public, interested in a certain nation-wide community of news statement and discussion.

Another incident of this tendency to enlargement and concentration is the crowding out of independent small-scale publishing enterprises. To a certain extent, the size of the most efficient organ for mass communication is a function of the technical instruments available; and these today imply great costs and therefore extensive plants with a correspondingly broad base in their public. So far as this is the case, only large organizations can survive as carrying the main burden of the industry. They compete with each other; but lesser enterprises tend to exist only in their shadow, not as competitors, but as local supplements.

Due partly to this cause, and partly to the simple arithmetic of national growth, it is less and less true that every American with something to say can find his way to the hearing of *all* the people. In a group of a hundred people, everybody—given time and patience—can both speak and listen to everybody else. In a group of a thousand, since listening capacity while extensible is not infinite, this is no longer physically possible. As the group increases in number, the percentage of the whole that can be heard by all becomes smaller. If every thought of every mind could make its way through print and radio to every other, the appalling flood would smother the possibility of a hearing for any. The lessening proportion of Americans who can gain a national hearing is not of itself a calamity; it is but another way of describing the wealth of thought-output of a hundred million minds.

It follows that the right to speak and print does not carry with it a right of access to the ears of a nation, nor indeed to anyone's ears unless he is willing. The rights of listeners will engage us in detail later on;[8] at the moment only these two facts concern us: that the listener needs a wide variety to choose from and that he needs a rigorous selection of those who claim a hearing from the

8. See below, chap. 5.

entire public. The right of every individual to speak must remain inviolate; also his right to print and distribute to such audience as he can rouse. But he cannot claim as a right access to the clientele of any existing medium; he cannot demand of right that his letter be printed. Still less has he a right to time on the radio. Is he then injured, or is society injured, by the lessening number of the larger press services?

There is certainly a smaller proportion of chief editors for him to appeal to. On the other hand, each of them—on an average—reaches a larger fraction of the nation. Unless the great organizations were there, those who after selection might claim access to them would be helpless to reach their due audience, and both they and the public would be cheated. The interest of free speech requires as its perfect equipment the nation-wide press, such as does not yet exist, though from the technological point of view it is already within reach. For ideal freedom the organizational spread should be greater and not less, so far as the *equipment of freedom,* its positive factor, is concerned.[9] Under existing circumstances, however, this spread, if it were achieved by further consolidation, might very probably be achieved at the cost of impoverishing another and indispensable element of freedom, *a sufficiently typical variety of editorial policies.* It is not, of course, a question of the actual number of news sources—there could easily be too many—it is a question of the *representative character* of their spread of opinion, and equally of mood and level. If there were no equivalent of *Punch*—and I am not saying there is— the American press would lack typical variety.

9. See above, p. 54.

On this point of variety we have to distinguish between the press available to already known group interests and causes and the press available to as yet unknown or struggling new ideas. In regard to the former, the known minorities, groups, causes—all of them, so far as I know them, already have a press, though few consider their own press "proportionate" or "adequate." There are two reasons, apart from the formidable financial obstacle to greatness, why the press of these groups is weaker than the groups themselves. The first is the old law, to him that hath shall be given: any majority press, having a large base of support, can offer the best services, and therefore wins from the smaller groups; whereas there is no assurance that, even with great capital outlay, the smaller group could win the majority away from its accustomed provender. The second reason is the divided mind of the smaller group toward its own press. It wishes indeed to interpret the world to its own people in its own way; but it also, and very particularly, wishes this interpretation to reach the rest of the community. But this it can do only through using the already existing major press as its vehicle; unless by some exceptional merit (as the *Christian Science Monitor* does) it can extend itself into the field of the major press also. So far, then, as we have to deal with known interests, such as labor, agriculture, religion, the variety is all there; nothing is without a press; it is the proportion that is lacking. As for the unknown or struggling causes, they may appear at any point in the social order; and certainly, the larger the number of editorial heads, the better their chances of finding shelter during infancy. Besides, the purely personal variety of editorial heads may at any time furnish the needed ally to the feeble side of a new social issue. On these grounds, though speculative, the cause of variety requires special concern for the minor and local press.

Effective freedom thus requires both a typical diversity not yet proportionately attained (though I am not sure how proportion is measured) and a totality of spread only sketchily realized; the two requirements appear inconsistent, though in fact they are not. Their reconciliation will depend less on what the individual freedom of expression calls for than on what the public needs and can use. Individual freedom appears to be served by untrammeled expression; but the unordered multiplicity of voices in simultaneous conspiracy for attention serves no one, the individual speaker least of all. If he wants the public ear, he wishes to get it through means which do not affront and confuse the public mind and which assure him respect when his turn arrives, and that means through systematized channels of selection. That which is open to all without condition commands and deserves no public deference.

The chief obstacle to free access to suitable media, in the American press, may prove to be less an inadequate variety of the media themselves than arbitrary exclusions by existing editors. There is many a good American writer who cannot get his ideas printed in the existing *major* press. Not even a columnist whose column is bought and paid for can legally compel an editor to print what he has written. The position of editors might become impossible if he could; yet there are moral rights which limit the editor's privilege of exclusion. With all the weeding-out of worthless stuff which is necessary, there exist definite injuries to writers and definite losses to the American public. What the writer and the public have a moral right to demand is that the editor's selection be made in the interest of the American people and not solely on the basis of personal crotchet, the protection of a pet cause, or even editorial policy. (It might, of course, be difficult for the editor himself to make this distinction!)

The local press is an opportunity for the tryout of local talent; it is not a substitute for the national press, nor the national press for it. Its survival is a matter of importance; it will be secured by a recognized differentiation of function.

At the moment, the local press, and particularly the weekly with rural circulation, is in a position of peculiar strain. Its financial basis, always precarious, is threatened by radio and other news services. Its neediness renders it susceptible to the inducements of aid through syndicated material supplied free or for small charges by interests with axes to grind and through advertisements well paid for. So far as these inducements are effective, the independence of the grass roots of opinion is attacked at its weakest point. If financial strength renders mental independence of the press difficult, financial weakness renders it vulnerable.

Here, again, the problem of a free press is not solely one of the rights of personal utterance; it is also a problem of what the public has a right to expect.

27. DANGERS FROM RESTRICTED ACCESS TO FACT

Freedom to speak and print assumes that the issuer has something to convey. His freedom is that of giving currency to what is already in him as part of his mental property, whether of information or of opinion. It would appear on the face of it absurd to suggest that this freedom includes a right to publish ideas or facts of which the proposed issuer *is not in possession*. Yet a recent decision of the Supreme Court implies in certain cases such a right. It holds that news media cannot be arbitrarily excluded from the facilities to command possession of and to print news which they have not gathered, but which has been gained by the costly efforts of an international news agency. Whatever the legal aspects of this case, brought under the Sherman Act, certainly the First Amendment did not contemplate as essential to a free press an effective claim of right to purchase information gathered by others.[10]

But the reasoning on which this decision is supported, so far as it touches on the meaning of press freedom, is not based on the primary and commonly understood right of expressors to express; it is based on another demand, the need of the public as consumer of news to be well served.[11] This necessity or right of the public,

10. *Here the conflict seems to be between two forms of press liberty, the would-be subscriber's being of the sort hinging on "command of means" (see above, p. 54, l. 24). The trouble seems to be that the First Amendment does not protect this latter form of liberty against private refusal to furnish service—such protection requires governmental action at the expense of the other form, and it is against governmental action only that the First Amendment literally runs. So the doctrine of restraint of trade may be a more pertinent alternative, as against stretching the meaning of the First Amendment, if this "command of means" is to be protected. Cf. p. 162, last whole paragraph.—*CLARK.

11. *Judge Learned Hand in the case above cited* (U.S. *v.* Associated Press, 52 Fed. Sup. 372): "*Neither exclusively, nor even primarily, are the interests of the newspaper industry conclusive;*

if indeed it extends to a right to gather in the public interest "where it hath not strawed," claiming access to information as yet unknown to the utterer, is a right of the highest importance. It can plausibly be said that, since no act is free unless it is adequately equipped, no regular *function* of expression is free unless it is supplied from whatever source with the stuff which is to be expressed. This would give something like a lien upon whoever is in possession of information important to the public to deliver it, with or without a price, to the press. What, then, if the possessor of such knowledge is the government? If, as is often the case, government fails to avow policies or explain situations on which public judgment depends, shall the press be empowered to pry open the official oyster? Or if the possessor is a private individual who has not offered his knowledge for sale, does the superior claim of the press, resting on the public interest, override his rights of privacy and his privilege of nonexpression? If so, the present decision is indeed revolutionary in its scope.[12]

---

for that industry serves one of the most vital of all general interests; the dissemination of news from as many different sources and with as many different facets and colors as is possible . . . . to deprive a paper of any service of the first rating is to deprive the reading public of means of information which it should have."

12. *The decision was that the defendant had violated the Sherman Act. Judge Hand thought that the policy of the Sherman Act in this connection resembles the policy of the First Amendment. Black and Frankfurter agreed to some extent, though less explicitly. The amendment restrains only Congress and federal officials who are carrying out the will of Congress. It does not operate to restrain the Associated Press or any other private corporation. I do not know what would happen if Congress should deprive newspapers of the power to purchase the services of the Associated*

But the principles underlying these problems, as of the problems of concentration and diversity, have in each case carried us beyond the question of the rights of those who express to that of the rights of those who consume. This further question is the concern of our next chapter.

Press. The question here raised by Hocking as a philosophical question would then arise as a legal question. It is, of course, interesting, in advance of any such legal issue, to speculate about the moral right of freedom of the press, which may or may not include the right to purchase information gathered by others.— CHAFEE.

—This case is discussed more fully on pp. 170–73. I am concerned here not with the decision itself but with the reasonings whereby the two decisions (that of the district court of New York and that of the Supreme Court) were supported. These reasonings, as is usual with legal reasonings, strayed into philosophical territory; and since philosophy is here our business, we become at once concerned with their implications. In my view, these implications cannot be left unchallenged. The press must have some right to pry oysters open, including perhaps the A.P. oyster. On the other hand, government, and occasionally private persons, must have some right to keep the oyster shut. The boundary between these conflicting rights is at present undetermined; I am here pointing out the significance of the issue.—W. E. H.

5

FREEDOM OF THE PRESS AS AFFECT-
ED BY INTERESTS OF COMMU-
NITY AND CONSUMER

THE press today is no longer primarily a means of expression for thinkers. In their hold on the interests of readers, editorial opinions retreat in comparative importance before other contents of the press vehicle of which *the news* may stand as a symbol. The crude fact is that, while many people choose their paper on account of its editorial policy, few buy it because of its editorials. The news, when it is the report of facts which it pretends to be, is less a medium for the views of the issuer than a necessary grist for the thinking of the reader. This is a service for which he will pay, as he will not ordinarily pay the man who claims freedom to express his mind. Freedom of the press cannot be discussed today solely on the basis of the rights of free expression for the producers of opinion.

It is true that in all freedom of speech the listener is assumed to exist. The right to speak, as a privilege to utter words in solitude, has never been disputed nor claimed; there are always at least two parties in the picture, though only one of them is the claimant of right. What that claimant is interested in is the opportunity to get his ideas *across*, and into another mind, it being taken for granted that he has found or can find somebody to hear him. The speaker has no right to compel a hearing; there could be no right of free speech if there were not a corresponding right not to listen. It would hardly do to make free speech free and listening compulsory, though that might be the speaker's dream![1] The existence of an audience is thus a sign that the speech does to some extent serve an interest of the listeners.

Let us call these two parties the *issuer* and the *consumer*.[2] The press, in the wide meaning we are giving it, to include book, magazine, radio, film, etc., is the issuer of news and opinions. The readers and hearers are the consumers of news and opinions or, collectively, the *audience*.[3]

1. *This is doubtless why men become professors.*—HUTCHINS.

2. *These terms are not too happy. The "consumer" does not exclusively possess what he purchases nor devour it without selection and without response. Press service is in form a one-way process of transfer, but in intention a two-way process of stimulus and reaction.*

Further, wherever there are two parties within a community, there is always a third party, the community itself—in this case vitally concerned with the impact of all communication on both parties, on the social fabric, and on the standards which measure the free cohesion of the group. It is for the sake of throwing into relief the involvement of this third party that we here limit our analysis to the bare dual relationship of speaker and listener.

3. *I would argue, as MacLeish has done in the Commission's meetings, for the recognition of a third party, the individual who has something to say but no press with which to say it. He is quite commonly the "source" of opinion, mentioned in Hocking's succeeding paragraph. In his freedom to induce a press medium to publish his material, the First Amendment protects him, as it protects the press owner, against governmental interference. To that extent he has a legal right, protected mainly through protecting the publisher, though in conceivable circumstances the individual*

162

As the issuer cannot compel an audience, so the consumer cannot compel the existence of a speaker. Nor does it usually occur to him that he has a claim upon anyone for more light and leading than is spontaneously offered. The expresser is offering a gift. Nevertheless, the consumer is not a passive receptacle. Since the issuer cannot survive without his free attention, the consumer has power to encourage or discourage his advances. Through the consumer's willingness to pay for the succesful divination of his appetites, he lures out the yield of thought-products; it is his free suffrage that builds up the great press and sustains a mass production in which thought and pseudo-thought devised for the market mix in varying proportions. He may go to the extent of setting up, with a like-minded group, a press organ to meet special group needs, interests, or prejudices; here the con-

---

might have ground of action. I would argue that he has a moral right to more than this, on Hocking's grounds. Hocking designates it as an important interest but not a right (p. 186, n. 18).

The individual with something to say has a duty, and therefore a right, to speak. He has a duty, and therefore a right, to reach the larger audience that goes with publication (implying provision of appropriate means) if his material would add to the effective mental grist of that larger audience. It would seem to follow that he has a "right" to an honest and objective judgment, in the public interest, as to whether his material meets this test. This could hardly be made a legal right; it remains therefore a moral one, imposing a corresponding moral duty on the publishers of existing press media. Infallibility being out of the question, this amounts to a duty to curb their personal and economic biases in deciding such matters.—CLARK.

—Though I go somewhat less than the full way with MacLeish, as noted above (pp. 98–99), and Clark agrees with MacLeish, I continue to think that Clark and I emerge at much the same point.—W. E. H.

sumer controls, or perhaps becomes, the issuer. But the
birth of opinion the consumer cannot control; the genesis
of thought is incurably free and individual. For its
abundance and pertinence he must take his chances as
with the fertility of his native soil. He is necessarily interested in the freedom of the sources of opinion, because if
they are unchecked and unwarped, even by himself, he
will have, other things being equal,[4] the widest and most
honest offering to select from or to piece together or to
mix with his own thought. His interest here coincides
with that of the issuer, actual or potential.

Hence, though there are two distinct interests, only
one of them, in simple conditions, needs protection; to
protect the issuer is to protect the consumer.

But if through a decrease in the relative number or
variety of sources, or a growing imperativeness of the
consumer's need, or both, the freedom not to listen were
to vanish, then to protect the interest of the issuer only
would no longer be sufficient. The press would be clothed
with a new responsibility, since the other of the two
parties would be bound. This, broadly speaking, is the
situation today. Through concentration of ownership,
the available variety of news sources in many communities has declined. At the same time the insistency of the
consumer's need has universally increased. It is true that
today I am as free not to buy a paper as not to listen
to a speech—but only because there are other sources of

4. *That the total offering may be too wide for the consumer's
oversight, and that he may lose truth through its very abundance,
is a point which present experience strongly urges on our consideration, though it has as yet had no attention from our social
theorists. All the classic arguments assume that the chances of
getting truth increase with the volume and variety of the offerings.*

news; the news per se I am no longer free not to consume. This fact indicates a new importance in the news function and a new responsibility in the work of the reporter which is not yet adequately reflected in his social and economic status.[5]

The importance of this news function is obscured by the bulk of material carried by the press which has and claims no necessity; much of it is convenience or amusement, some of it is addiction. The typical news medium of today is a magazine in the original sense—a department store; there is entertainment, criticism of art and music, directory to the passing show, advertising lure and

5. *This new responsibility is reflected in remarks attributed to Mr. Alexander Kendrick in the form of advice to reporters on the eve of his recent assignment to the Soviet Union:*

"Don't give the editor what he wants. He doesn't know what he wants. You're the man on the scene and you have to call your own shots. In most cases the editor suffers from over-reading. He reads too many other stories. . . . . He gets preconceptions. The clever reporter used to be the one that satisfied his editor's preconceptions. But it doesn't work that way any more. The competent reporter is now the man who satisfies his editor's urge to know, and the only way to do that is to write stories that answer questions and explain situations for your own mind.

"Don't be condescending. . . . .

"Don't generalize. This is usually an editorial rather than a reportorial fault, but American correspondents in Russia have been guilty of it. You can't make a flat statement about all Russians any more than about all Americans. You can't make flat statements about Soviet policy or Soviet planning or Soviet intentions. . . . .

"Forget about Dostoievsky. . . . . Of course there are brooding Russians just as there are brooding Nebraskans. . . . .

"Assumed in all this is that the reporter is qualified for his job, that he has some knowledge of Russian history and culture, that he is aware of the great importance of his assignment as an essay in understanding, and that he wants to do the job well . . . ." (Reporter *[New York], October, 1945).*

market report; there is sustenance for various group interests lively enough to float a column—always Sport, Women, Society, Health, Cuisine, sometimes Science, Building, Labor, Chess..... Mingling with this floating gazetteer of Current Culture and its personnel there is a Fictional Bait, the serials in word and picture whose interest is the effortless exercise of the elementary social judgments upon unwearying and ageless character symbols, while for the newssheet their value is the hook of dramatic tension in ceaseless continuity. In all this the Mind of the Time is being exhibited to Each Mind for such *smörgåsbord* as suits him; as the spiritual aura of the news, it is all news. It is information and the value scheme which enwraps information. Through it the press exercises a definite educational function, for, in supplying an assumed demand, it affects the level of public taste and interest for better or for worse; consumption is never static.

In any case, through this enormous labor and through the news columns proper, there is being brought to the reader a part of his life, something to actualize and make graphic his membership in the living world, something in the nature of daily bread for his mental activities as a social being and as a citizen. It is a need, not a convenience. It has become a need largely through what the press itself has made possible; contemporary man exists in an immeasurably extended environment—his needed breath-of-air may be ten thousand miles away. Having made a world of world-breathers, communication has lost its right not to serve them; it is bound by its own success. We shall be concerned with the rights and duties determined by this human need.

166

28. THE FUNCTIONS OF THE PRESS, TYPIFIED BY THE NEWS FUNCTION, ARE "CLOTHED WITH A PUBLIC INTEREST"

Whenever an institutional activity affects a general need, there is a public concern that the effect be favorable rather than detrimental. One begins to speak of a "right" of the public to have its news; this language has no necessary legal implications—a moral right lifts its head to announce an answering responsibility on the part of the institution. The support of the alleged right will depend on the depth of the public concern. In the case of the press, the concern goes deep; society is concerned for the cultural versatility of its members, for the depth and variety of experience shared by all; it is increasingly important that mental explorations within a nation should become a joint and simultaneous adventure; science becomes front-page news by necessity. The homogeneity of nations involved in technological advance would be impaired without the incessant flow of report and its universal distribution.

Beyond this there is a definite political concern. The news content of the press enters at once into the thought-processes of the public. To provide the data for *an ideally independent* judgment of public affairs, the news would have to be unwarped by editorial opinion; the reader would have to be able to start where the editor starts, with the day's income of unslanted fact in all its crudity, bulk, and fragmentary puzzledom. As this is obviously impossible, such independence is one of the unattainable ideals; yet its substance remains as a goal. It is unattainable because condensed reports are necessarily interpreted reports and also because few readers are robust

167

enough to find without aid what the facts mean. But it remains as an inescapable goal because only to the extent that the reader gains contact with the raw stuff on which judgment is based is he a wholly free judge. If his schooling has given him an intimation of how such raw material is transformed into a "story," he has at least a clue to a free reading of the news text.[6]

A reader of news for the day's interest may be merely receptive; a reader of news as a citizen cannot be a passive reader. He must be making up his mind, as if he were responding to the voice of the press in a two-way activity. In an authoritarian society where the news and its meaning are dispensed together, this return action is not called for: the citizen echoes the interpretation of the news source. In a free community the citizen is given the wherewithal to differ; he responds with his own reflections built upon his own data. No one does this amount of original thinking in regard to all the news; but everyone is assumed to have the data in hand for such original thinking as he is disposed and able to do: it is an entire community of varying minds which the press must serve with its raw material for thought. The fulness and unbent integrity of the news thus becomes a profound social concern. That which is a necessary condition of performing a duty is a right; we may therefore speak of the moral right of a people to be well served by its press. The addressee of this right is in the first instance the press itself: its responsibility is measured by the fact that, as the data required for the functions of citizenship are widely dispersed in space and time,

6. *Some exercise of this sort might enter into the training in reading we were talking about (p. 149).*

a vanishing proportion of them is open to anyone's direct observation; a people is almost wholly dependent on its press for the primary data of its political thinking.

But, since the citizen's *political* duty is at stake, the right to have an adequate service of news becomes a *public responsibility* as well. The phrase "freedom of the press" must now cover two sets of rights and not one only. With the rights of editors and publishers to express themselves there must be associated a right of the public to be served with a substantial and honest basis of fact for its judgments of public affairs. Of these two, it is the latter which today tends to take precedence in importance; in Robert Leigh's pertinent phrase, freedom of the press "has changed its point of focus from the editor to the citizen." It is even necessary, in an age dominated by the social interest, to make an effort to remember that the editor is still there and that his freedom to utter opinion is, so to speak, the first charge of the phrase "freedom of the press."[7]

This freedom has always been a matter of public as well as individual importance. Inseparable from the right of the press to be free has been the right of the people to have a free press. But the public interest has advanced beyond that point; it is now the right of the people to have *an adequate press*. (Is this an impossible or meaningless demand? We shall inquire.) It is not sufficient that what is in the press shall be the untrammeled utterance of the issuers; the press in its own

7. *One motive for the division in this text between chaps. 3 and 5 is to emphasize this distinction and to protect in a phase of history swamped with social aspects the essential individualism of the sources of thought in which the fertility as well as the virility of our civilization is vested.*

169

growth has moved in upon a vital function in community life, and, finding itself there, is confronted with the new necessity of fulfilling that function. Its activities are "affected by a public interest"; and the task of practical action as well as of theory is to take the measure of that interest, and its ensuing obligations. The freedom of the publisher to publish becomes responsible to a specific public goal. The editors do not thereby lose their primary liberty to write and publish whatever they think; they *may lose the liberty*, if it is such, *to fail* in the task of connecting the minds of their readers with the going currents of fact, thought, and feeling in the world of their membership.

29. THE APPARENT LEGAL STATUS OF THIS PUBLIC INTEREST: IS THE PRESS IN SOME SENSE A COMMON CARRIER?

We say that the public has a right to an adequate press and that the press has a duty to be adequate. Is this right-and-duty pair legal or, as we sometimes say, merely moral?

"Adequacy" is an indefinite standard. We imagine on one side a body of readers or listeners, and in the wide world beyond their observation a vague body of factual truth, thought, emotional upheaval over "issues" in which God knows what human values are being tried out—a formless totality because unbounded—with which that body of readers or listeners needs to be in liaison. We say recklessly that they have "a right to know"; yet it is a right which they are helpless to claim, for they do not know that they have the right to know what as yet they do not know. In a sense, whatever they are told by the efforts of other people is pure gratuity. The press is always more than we deserve. Adequacy is always more or less attained in the remarkable achievements of the energy of the contemporary press. At the same time it is always a more or less distant goal, a fact which the press knows better than its readers; perhaps a goal literally out of human reach. It might seem, then, that the right of the public in press performance must remain a moral claim rather than a definable legal requirement.

However, in the important case above referred to, *United States* v. *Associated Press* (326 U.S. 20), the Supreme Court appears to have set general press responsibility into our fundamental law, professing to find it in the implications of the First Amendment. The case itself hardly seems to involve the general theory of the press; it merely deals with a special and commercially plausible restriction of access to news already gathered; the decision condemns this restriction as a restraint of trade. But the reasoning through which this restriction is found illegal enwraps the whole work of the press in a public interest publicly guaranteed.

Mr. Justice Black, who wrote the majority opinion, sees "the welfare of the public" as the central issue; he finds this welfare the concern of the First Amendment inasmuch as "a free press is a condition of a free society." He argues that "freedom to publish . . . . guaranteed by the Constitution" would be inconsistent with a "freedom to combine to keep others from publishing."[8] This argument is sharpened in the language of a supporting

8. *If this is intended as a summary of the purpose of A.P., it can only be characterized as highly inaccurate.*

opinion: "A free press is indispensable to the workings of our democratic society. The business of the press, *and therefore* the business of the Associated Press, is the promotion of truth regarding public matters by furnishing a basis for the understanding of them. . . . . A public interest so essential to the vitality of our democratic government may be defeated by private restraints no less than by public ownership."[9] And the inference is that the Court will interpret existing law as adequate to restrain any such restraints to "the promotion of truth," etc.

It is not clear from the opinions in this case how far the Court is prepared to go beyond this somewhat negative obligation of government to restrain restraints on the free flow of ideas. Is it prepared to uphold positive standards of performance?

The fundamental acknowledgment that press functions are now, in the eyes of the law as well as of common sense, "clothed with a public interest" suggests an affirmative obligation on the part of government. But the phrase by much use has become ambiguous within the law; and while Judge Learned Hand, in the original federal suit in the district court of New York, uttered the word "regulation,"[10] nothing so vigorous is involved in

9. *Mr. Justice Frankfurter. (My italics.) It is solely the affirmative element in this statement that here concerns us. In the extremely loose reasoning which marks most of the opinions in this case, the original concern of the Bill of Rights for individual liberties is wholly ignored.*

10. *Judge Hand denounced the phrase "clothed with a public interest" as a verbal debating ground tending to obscure the real issue. He proposed as the direct way to get at the substance of the matter to consider "the public importance of the activity." His test is that "when the public aspect of the activity prevails . . . .*

the Supreme Court decision. The question reverts to our own hands, as we now inquire what social and governmental obligations ought to be recognized.

In considering this question, it will be helpful to recall analogous private activities in which affirmative action of government is accepted as called for. The media of mass communication are in a position very imperfectly analogous to that of a common carrier. Press associations for news-gathering, however, especially since not many of them can be tolerated in their activities at any one point on the planet, may well as they approach monopoly be regarded as common carriers in the sense that their services ought to be available to all who are prepared to pay for them at market rates. There is no such approach to monopoly in press functions as a whole. Yet the tendency to concentration of control in a few hands (as well as the distinct advantages of large-scale operations) is bound to raise the question whether, in particular cases, the character of common carrier is not in fact being assumed; and whether, therefore, the responsibilities associated with that concept should not be required. There are, however, closer and more helpful analogies.

---

in administering the Anti-Trust Act courts must so declare." To show how simple the whole matter is, he quotes with approval an opinion in Nebbia v. New York (291 U.S. 502): *"If one embarks in a business which public interest demands shall be regulated, he must know regulation will ensue!" It is not clear, however, that either Judge Hand or the Supreme Court is prepared to advise "regulation" as a corollary of the public interest in the work of the press. We may perhaps draw the inference that neither would regard regulation as illegitimate if it were shown necessary to secure the required performance.*

The press is more closely like a public utility in private hands. It is still more like a system of private schools undertaking through personal initiative to perform a function which is distinctly a public concern. What experience has shown in both these cases is that the public interest does not take care of itself through the spontaneous play of private interests and ambitions alone. Some positive assertion of the public interest by government has been required. In the case of the schools, private enterprise failed at the important point of equalizing opportunity; the state enters not to regulate but to do a supplementary job, and to do it on a nationwide scale which tends partially to displace the private institutions. The argument seems to be that primary education is too vital to the success of a democratic government to be left to the chances of private purses and inclinations; the whole nation must tax itself to educate all the children. This argument might conceivably be transferred to the functions of the press in its expanded powers. We note that there is no item in the Bill of Rights guaranteeing the freedom of the schools. Have the schools lost their freedom in being publicly operated? Would the press under analogous treatment remain free? And would the public be better served? These are not living issues with us; but it belongs to the logic of our inquiry to consider why this is the case.

30. THE PUBLIC INTEREST IN THE FUNCTIONS OF SCHOOL AND PRESS CANNOT BE SECURED WITHOUT A BASIS OF PRIVATE ENTERPRISE

Such success as our public schools have achieved is due partly to these circumstances: that the materials of

primary instruction can and should have a nation-wide
uniformity; that the subject matter of this instruction is
irrelevant to the concerns of party politics; and that the
public schools are never the whole of primary education,
being flanked by two normally effective educational
agencies, the home and the church. These two agencies
are incurably private and personal; the separation between church and state is a matter of political principle
with us, and the separation of home and state so rooted
in habit that no one ever thinks to assert it. What we observe today is, that as home and church become derelict
in their part, especially the moral part, of the educational
task, the public school shows itself incapable of carrying the whole load. What the state needs from the schools
is the development of citizens understanding and attached to the democratic order; what it begins to get
and must increasingly get as home and church limp in
their moral support, is a crop of democratic parrots, and
from its own resources alone the state can produce
nothing else. For *the state cannot educate.*[11] What it can
do is to select and organize educators and keep its
political biases strictly out of this work. By a remarkable, and I think instinctive, self-limitation, our various
state and municipal governments have observed an ap-
proximate working separation of school and state in
regard to the direct business of teaching; though through
the budgets and appointments the political will exerts
a disturbing and sometimes corrupting influence. To the

11. *The state must include in its total purpose its own continued renewal, hence the education of its citizens; it must see to
it that this essentially spiritual task is fulfilled through home,
church, and school by persons and processes free from its own
intrusion, obeying the intrinsic laws of thought and culture.*

extent that the state dictates methods and the specific content of education, the schools fail to educate.

The first instruction to be drawn from this analogy for the press is on this negative point; as the state cannot educate, so also the *state cannot edit the news*.[12] The processes are not radically dissimilar; both require a breath of life from inside which cannot be commanded or ordered by rule. No doubt, as in the public schools, the state could select and organize newsmen to do their own editing and adopt a self-denying ordinance for their freedom. But the work of the press demands an art and a variety not possible in the schools; whatever the state might do, an independent press must be beside it. There are standards of press performance; but the work of preparing the stuff for the press can never be standardized. The scenting-out and unearthing of news, its selection and mounting, is an infinite task; it is not reducible to an official activity or to any single activity. The perception of the relative significance of events in the endless multitude of happenings, the conveying of their emo-

12. *This statement is objected to, and with some justice, on the ground of excess. There is a degree of hyperbole in saying that the state cannot edit the news when it obviously does edit a certain amount of the news, both in its handouts to the press and in its own communiqués on current political and military happenings.*

The meaning of the assertion is that the state cannot do the editing of the news as a political function, replacing the efforts of private agencies, as explained below (p. 177). The state likewise cannot do sculpture, and there are few sadder objects in the land than monuments too closely shaped by official specification; nevertheless, the public monument is a necessary and important field for the free work of an artist under government commission. Government must find, employ, and respect the artist. The analogy with government news service is close, for art also is a mode of expression.

176

tional quality which is a part of the truth of the story, the prophetic discernment in the obscure trends of to-day of what is going to be important tomorrow—all these call for the intuitions of free and individual observers. The variety of these observers must correspond to the variety of the types of public questioning: the reporter is the vicarious eye and ear of a mind at home; that mind is in search of a voice which responds to events some-what as he himself is inclined to respond to them. The reporter of news, the writer of dispatches, is dealing in-tuitively—like the teacher—with questions he has not heard. The more summary a news report has to be, the more it is a work of personal judgment and art to report it.

And as for the standards which the result of this work must reach, and which directly concern public welfare, they present the extraordinary embarrassment for public administration of being—at least some of them—not alone indefinite but contradictory. The news, we say, must be adequate; that means, it must be full: but also it must not be confusing. When is the news "full"? Since there is no such totality as "all the news," since no reader could use it if he had it, and since anything short of the whole must be selected by unwritten principles such as no bureau could tolerate, there is no possibility of a perfect performance. The ambition to fill out detail must be checked by the necessities of emphasis and the danger of giving nothing in giving too much. As John Grierson has put it, "The high duty of reducing bewilderment and establishing patterns of thought and feeling takes prece-dence of 'all the facts that are fit to print.'" Or, again, the news must be objective and factual, free from inter-pretative bias; and yet it must make sense, and, if the

177

emotional aura is omitted, the facts present a falsehood. What the facts, as reported in still photographs, never convey is the sense of direction, and the urge which attaches itself to an invisible, a nonexistent future goal; yet the direction and velocity and insistence are the realities:[13] where a man is not but wants to be is commonly far more important than where he is. The reporter who substitutes romance for fact runs an awful risk of lying; but the reporter who offers the facts without their inherent romance is surely lying. These contradictory requirements must be united as life, not office rules, can unite them; and the results must be addressed to the concrete audience by one who knows what that particular audience is ready for and what requires an initiation. These considerations need not be called pedagogical, but literally that is what they are; it is *because* the state cannot teach that it cannot edit the news. The field is one for competitive enterprise; because there is no perfect teacher and no perfect solution, the effort must be manifold and recurrent and individual, always open to imaginative advance.

The argument does not imply that the state is powerless to aid the public interest in press service through any voice of its own, nor through the enlistment of ability developed in the free press to bring its own large share in the news to the people. It implies simply that the state cannot, for the sake of securing the public interest,

13. *As a detail, the press may and does occasionally falsify by suppressing the element of change and motion, as illustrated magazines achieve pornographic effects by presenting still-life attitudes of dancers, skaters, etc., which are dissolved in the actual performance—false to the emotion by being false to the motion.*

178

replace the independent press or take over the job as its monopoly without defeating the public interest. Even if the central political objection could be surmounted—that no government ought to be in a position to select for its citizens the facts upon which they must base their judgment of that government—the people would lose that vitality of the report which is their own mental vitality, and which springs from the inward life of the press observer which is his freedom of thought and intuition.

If we could imagine the state as organizing some part of the free talent of the press into a "public press system," on the analogy of the public school system, and for the same reason—namely, for the sake of equalizing for all the people access to the environing life of mankind—we could conceive certain gains as well as certain losses. The nation might be better served in the point of a uniformly respectable press service; further, there might be achieved one great desideratum now within technical reach, simultaneous publication in every part of the country. The voice of such an official press, or should we say established press, would have an appalling unanimity; it would save the people no end of confusion; it might eliminate many of the more scandalous departures from sanity, integrity, and decency; it would deal prudently with explosive foreign issues. But it would need to limit its own scope so as to maintain the ambition of the private press, and the power of that press to make one contribution of first-rate importance to the public interest, its leverage on government to yield its reserve on matters about which the people have a right to know.[14] In America, where custom is feeble, religion unsure of itself and divided, the mandarinate at a discount, the authority of the family vanishing, and the principles of right living reduced to a fading fashion by the enlightenment of moral relativity emanating from our higher learning, there are today only two powers in our society which can effectively criticize the state: business and the press.[15] The continuance of our effective freedom vis-à-vis government depends largely on bringing an independent press to do for the public interest what a public press system might be conceived to do for it.

31. HOW, THEN, CAN THE RESPONSIBILITY OF SOCIETY TOWARD THE RIGHTS OF THE NEWS-CONSUMING PUBLIC BE IMPLEMENTED?

The antithesis between complete laissez faire and complete governmental operation or control of the press is, for our society, unreal. A standard is not necessarily

14. *On October 19, 1945, an important political document relating to definite engagements made by President Roosevelt regarding our policies in the Near East was printed in the* New York Times. *The existence of that document had been denied by its official custodians. The denial of its existence led to the publication of the original in the Near East. Its publication there led to its official ackowledgment and publication here. Without the independent press, the public would have remained ignorant of the documentary basis of our present policy in that region, the letter from President Roosevelt to Ibn Saud. The point here is not the value of the policy; it is the value of a power to extract an avowal of policy.*

15. *Not labor?*—HUTCHINS.

—*Effective criticism of government must begin with a sense of community.*—W. E. H.

administered by government to be socially effective. A standard operates by its simple presence in consciousness; it will operate with increased effect if there are social agencies about for keeping it there. The press, like most other human enterprises, operates under a double set of standards of its own—its business standards and its professional standards of quality and public interest. The tendency of these two sets to a partial agreement leads to the illusion of coincidence, a common product of the will to believe. With or without external criticism, always abundant, the press is kept admonished of the more obvious desiderata. Its own ambition for technical excellence and for the range and pertinence of its news reports, sustained by American keenness, courage, and that penetrating drive whose shady side is a certain irreverence and disregard for the instinct of reserve, have made the American press the most efficient and speedy instrument of world coverage in history. In this result the profit motive has played a role; also the will to power through ideas, the desire to spread one's type of mind; also the instinct of workmanship and the enjoyment of the exercise of capacity—proportions variable and unknown! In the vigor of these motives, and the pressure of a competition for patronage, the press needs external support for its harder and less vocal lines of improvement.

By a slight stretch of language, we may call the self-judgment of the press by the press external; moments of review and self-criticism are external to the day's business. This is especially the case when such self-judgment is made the work of a specialized organ, a society, a journal, a school, in which professional standards are

181

discussed. Into such organs outside criticism penetrates and acquires a hearing. A more fully external judgment is the unorganized outcome of experience as the press interacts with other social agencies, a give-and-take in which abuses are revealed and to some extent corrected. If there were a specialized social organ for collating and announcing the upshot of such experience, enjoying the respect both of the press and of the public, the psychological effectiveness of standards would be greatly increased; at the same time the nature of the standards themselves would become clearer, and the line between the achievable and the impossible more evident. It is also within possibility that private agencies should maintain at important centers of event at home and abroad observers more highly qualified by training and human breadth and continuity of residence than the press services can usually send, and whose bulletins or reports could establish new standards of competence.

Diplomatic and consular representatives aboard are often well-informed, sometimes know the local language, and may stay long enough to understand what is happening around them; but as news sources they are ex officio partly muzzled. Is it inconceivable that a small group of men equally qualified, and locally in good standing, stationed at various critical points in the world, should be functionally unmuzzled, having the duty to put what they know to work at the right time and place? News from such sources might have a flavor of authenticity, sympathy, and justice —qualities not easily available to the professional rover.

Government remains the residuary legatee of responsibility for an adequate press performance. It is bound to consider whether self-administered standards and the normal self-righting elements within community life are sufficient to meet the public interest and eliminate emerging abuses. If they are not sufficient, government action may be indicated. It may take one or more of the following forms:

a) *Without intruding on press activities, the state may regulate the conditions under which those activities take place, so that the public interest is better served.*[16]— To make rules and conditions for a fairer game interferes with no honest freedom of the players; it improves the game for them and for the onlookers. To consider the total output of free press activity with analogous questions in mind might offer similar advantages both to the press and to its public. The ends in view would be the lessening of waste and disorder, the realizing of a genuine process of public thought, and the bringing of the best press service to the greatest number of people.

The best service to the most people! One natural defect of a commercial enterprise is the apportioning of service by ability to pay. In some lands where literacy is low, China, for example, radio has already found one way to correct this by making a universal and costless news service to some extent an actuality; a central receiving set in towns and villages and an adjacent bulletin board, read out by some literate to the crowd, give instant dissemination on a nation-wide scale of salient items. In America it is one of the great achievements of the free press that there is no one who cannot pay for a newspaper. But there is many a paper which cannot itself pay for the completest news service its subscribers could use; and there are millions of people who cannot procure at any price reasonably full news accounts on the day of issue because the major press still originates

16. See above, sec. 23, p. 130.

in single metropolitan centers. It may not be the function of government to correct this situation, so far as it is a domestic situation, on its own initiative; it would be its function to direct and perhaps aid private efforts toward its correction.[17]

The serving of representative variety is as much a public concern as an equable and nation-wide spread of service. But the thing is to make this variety contribute to public thought rather than to public division or public confusion. We say the state is concerned that public debate shall be real. Debate can be real only in proportion as the variety we speak of *enters the mind of each citizen,* rather than having each phase of the variety attended to solely by its own devotees. And this in turn requires that the variety—in so far as a nation-wide press exists or can be made to exist—shall appear *within that press.* Public debate through the usual editorial triumph over an absent and misrepresented opponent is a luxury which a democracy can no longer afford. The implied obligation of the press is accepted to some extent by many papers and by radio; it has now to be made a generally accepted standard and to be seen in what it does and does not demand.

It demands the actual confrontation of strong advocates. It does not demand proportionate representation of all views—the phrase is either meaningless or calls for the impossible. What is necessary is that each citizen be made aware, through participation in argument, that public issues involve genuine difficulties for honest men and not

17. *So far as private enterprise moves toward a national news and editorial service through consolidation, there are incidental dangers which we have earlier considered (p. 150).*

merely pretended difficulties camouflaging competing interests. It is not necessary for his guidance or consistent with the freedom of editors that the forum conception of debate should crowd out the force of advocacy or the right of an editor to his policy. Our public already knows that forums can be high debate, or indulgence in inconclusiveness, or even artificial alignments of speakers in the interest of a concealed advocacy; they see the merits of a firm and avowed but humane and tolerant side-taking. The nub of the matter is this: that anyone who fairly states any issue, from whatever angle, *must present the main alternative views*—otherwise what he states is not "the issue." Two or three able and reasonably just men will, as a rule, give a truer solidity to any public problem than a dozen such men. If the reader's mind can be engaged in a problem which already engages minds whom he respects, he will himself explore its various angles, and a genuine public thought-process will have begun.

The view that "the democratic process" is either insured or improved by the pure numerousness and variety of voices is a fallacy which I believe we are outgrowing. It is necessary to freedom of the press that no voice shall be suppressed or prevented from winning its own public; it is no part of freedom, it is neither desirable nor possible, that all receive an equal hearing, or a hearing by all.

There are other ways of advancing toward the reality of public debate than by moving toward a national press, obligated by its position to carry a representative variety of views. The local press might be aided to enlarge its news and editorial services to the point of what its public can be brought to use, until something like a local *New York Times* should blossom in every sizable city. An improved equivalent of the nation-wide bulletin service above referred to is quite within the reach of present wireless facilities; though a touch of the state might be required to guide the evolution.[18]

The editorial importance of the local press to the nation is so great that no course of development which should put the small paper to further financial disadvantage should be unchecked. It will probably require a touch of government to secure these three objects: the universal spread of what ought to be universal; a sturdy and adequate local press; and a fair hearing within each paper for a typical variety of opinion.

b) The state may extend the scope of present legal remedies, if a given type of abuse amounts to "poisoning the wells of public opinion."—If an injury to private reputation justifies limiting free expression by laws of libel and slander, an injury to the integrity of the news, certainly not less serious, would equally justify legal remedy, provided social remedies are inadequate and that more harm is not done by the remedy than by the injury.

In spite of the difficulties attending the legal effort to discourage press lying,[19] it is evident that flagrant and persistent distortion or falsification of evidence in

18. *The interest of the citizen who wants to get his views into the paper, a genuine and important interest though not a right, would not be perfectly served by a multiplication of local papers, unless his views relate to local matters. If they refer to a national problem and are worth printing, he wants to give them national publicity. But the multitude of the local press may be an important way stage to his goal.*

19. See above, pp. 110 and 115.

the press would most directly deserve the name of "poisoning the wells." It is intolerable that society should be without remedy for such abuse, merely because remedies are themselves open to abuse; to confess impotence on this ground alone is to retreat before the problem of distinguishing between malice and good will. The press itself has a powerful interest in preserving its repute against the cynicism growing in the public mind toward the reliability of the news. It would be freed rather than bound if there were usable legal means of ridding the profession of its worst practitioners. An on-guard attitude is salutary and is part of the education-by-experience of any democracy; but what we have today is a prevalent suspicion that news is tinctured with propaganda in the sinister sense of deliberate distortion or falsehood as contrasted with mistake or the allowable exaggeration of party zeal. Such suspicion reduces the value of the news and lames the original motive for building serious thinking upon it.

Without involving the state in the endless business of truth censorship, it would be possible to establish by law (i) a requirement of correction of a demonstrable falsehood (perhaps after the analogy of the German law of "Tatsächliche Berechtigung"),[20] and (ii), as we have suggested above, an extension of the purport of the concept of fraud to include instances of concealed purpose or concealed authorship in news statements or discussions of opinion.[21] It would also, I believe, be desirable that a proved purchase of opinion or news statement be

20. See Chafee, *Government and Mass Communications*, section on "Inaccuracy."

21. See above, p. 127.

punishable under laws relating to bribery, and involve the suspension of the offender from the practice of journalism.

Suppression of relevant evidence should be legally identified with falsification.

This Commission has recommended the establishment of a purely nongovernmental agency[22] for the continuous survey of press performance with respect to truth and fairness and for passing on the more flagrant cases of abuse. Such an agency would strengthen professional associations of the press in dealing with offenses against their own standards. In the main, the press has held a high standard of honor in the observance of secrecy regarding information given in confidence or held for release at a future time. There is no lack of a high professional pride in the press or of a clear sense of what needs to be done. It is all the more pertinent to inquire whether the law might not undertake, without involving itself in administering a professional license, to protect associations and agencies of review in the exercise of criticism and disciplinary action.

c) *The state may itself enter the field of news supply, not to compete with or to displace, but to supplement the yield of private agencies.*—The principle that a free government may not silence an opposition cannot be twisted to mean that a free government is prohibited from stating its own case, whether through its own organs or through use of space in the existing media.

The state is, in its nature, the greatest instrument for

22. See *A Free and Responsible Press: A General Report on Mass Communication: Newspapers, Radio, Motion Pictures, Magazines, and Books* (Chicago: University of Chicago Press, 1947), chap. 6.

achieving the common purposes of the human community.[23] It is an inherent absurdity to suppose that the state is prohibited from announcing, interpreting, and promoting those purposes by way of the instrumentalities of the press. It is a relic of an impoverished and suspicious view of the state to assume that its whole theory of the common good is limited to a minimal policing of individual activity; that it has nothing of its own to offer to the imagination, the hope, and the faith of the people beyond what is contained in the law. The state is the law, but it is also the maker of history and the maker of men; it is the liberating means to achievements of which they would otherwise be incapable. Its speech must convey the meaning of these objects; it owes this service to the floundering morale of our democratic societies. Nothing of the press, whether the printed word, the broadcast speech, the documentary or interpretative film, can be alien to its use.

Government—Congress, State Department, the Executive—as itself in sole possession of a great fund of information some of which the public "has a right to know" must be in the position of any speaker to control the extent and manner of the utterance of his own thought. The output of government printing offices is already a considerable fraction of the press product of a modern state. Press conferences are institutions which recognize the normality of flow of information into the privately established channels, as not alone the only existing channels through which the government can reach all the people in print, but perhaps better channels than gov-

23. On this point, see Hocking, *Man and the State*, chaps. xii and xxii.

ernmental sobriety, devoid of incidental seductions, would be able to create for itself. In principle, it is beyond doubt that press conversation with the public is a legitimate function of government.

But the press conference means something further, the right of the public to question government, and therefore the duty of government to answer, via the press. It is the American version of interpellation in Parliament. It would be an impossible institution if it were not for the recognized right of government to keep silent, where silence is dictated by public policy; no government could sustain such a relationship unless the necessities of discretion were mutually understood. All the more it is unnecessary for any government to maintain a deceitful façade which professes candor and practices blindfolding. The dictatorial government makes no pretense to answer questions: it suppresses truth and admits that it does so; the suppression of needed truth by a democratic government is a more sinister form of dictation because it also conceals the fact that it is being practiced. Distortion of truth by omission is a negative form of lying; and one value of the press conference is that this type of duplicity is rendered difficult.

Neither the value nor the necessity of governmental publication is neutralized by the fact that every government has its line and that in this sense all governmental expression is likely to fall under the shadow of policy. If a policy is malign, governmental expression becomes "propaganda"; if it is not, policy does not necessarily destroy its objectivity—it merely robs that expression of personal vitality, because it has to be the voice of a composite personality. The repute of a government with its own people or others is not different from that of a person; its particular coefficient of veracity becomes recognized, as one learns the degree of credence to be placed in the war communiqués of different nations. And, like a person, the fact that discounts will be made cannot suspend the obligation to speak, where it exists.

In international communications there exists this obligation in a conspicuous degree, because information has become a factor in world peace. What commercial agencies cannot do, government dare not allow to be undone, or to be done by other hands. If "the social need for international exchange of information . . . . cannot be filled by commercial agencies acting alone,"[24] the government has no choice but to become a colleague of the press in its own field, not to compete, but to hold a position until or unless the private agencies can take over.

The same logic would justify governmental pioneering in maintaining the adequacy of news service in the domestic area, where private agencies are not prepared to do the job.

d) *The state may make a strictly limited use of censorship.*—The evils of censorship are notorious. There are also evils of no censorship. Difficult as its function is, its danger lies not in the theoretical impertinence of governmental action to protect social standards but in the incidents of fallible judgment inseparable from human and personal administration. If this were a final objection, it would weigh as heavily against the practice of medicine. Censorship is not education; it is a check on

24. See report of White and Leigh, entitled *Peoples Speaking to Peoples* (Chicago: University of Chicago Press, 1946), p. 45, published by the Commission.

diseducation. It has to recognize in the press the plausible treasons to the slow civilizing of man. If obscenity always offended, it would need no censor; it is when obscenity seduces that it needs a censor. The obscene in press or stage comes forward assuming its own acceptability and does find acceptance among its own and a reliable market.

The social consequences are at first intangible; this is one of the difficulties in the community's position. If it attempts to define its objection to the "freedom to degrade"[25] in terms usable at law, it tends to fall back on such criteria as "a tendency to promote antisocial conduct." How can such a tendency be demonstrated? The effects of overemphasis on sex motives, of the destruction of reticence and normal shame, of the malodorous realism which claims superior candor and novelty for its rediscovery that man is an animal—what are the effects? Nothing at all that any eye can see; nothing but the slow unbalancing of emotion in the accepting mind, the disintegration of personality, the decay of taste, the gradual confirmation in the individual case of the hypothesis put before him that man is an animal—and nothing else. The devil of it is that a man who absorbs that hypothesis sufficiently can make it true; and what law can punish the infiltration of "truth" into the soul? It is this sly and pervasive hypocrisy of vice, its honorless campaign under cover of fine words against the most fragile defenses of the soul, and especially of the soul of youth, that makes the community's case so difficult, the path of the law so obscure, and the work of the cen-

25. See above, p. 48.

sor so severe, so thankless, so beset with the terror of mistake.

The alternative is to throw up the sponge and talk about "self-righting processes," and the "normal instinct of sound mankind," the shock-absorbing capacities of "the adult mind," the improvements in genuine morality which attend greater frankness all around and "a little greater freedom in these matters." Then what if the self-righting does not take place, and the total picture of your community seen in quietude is one of a disoriented moral sense—shall we say of a pervasive, genial, inwardly tragic inebriety? Is passivity the answer? A community which passively accepts this traffic must also accept the inference from its inaction: that this community is a place in which decadence will be unopposed because it cannot be defined and in which obscenity is an uncontested source of recreation—No Protest! The censor merely registers a caveat. And it should be hard for a democracy to confess inability to sustain its own standards because judicious organs of censorship cannot be had.

6

THE ENDURING GOAL AND THE
VARIABLE REALIZATION

A FREE press is not a passing goal of human society;
it is a necessary goal. For the press, taken in sum,
is the swift self-expression of the experience of each
moment of history; and this expression ought to be true.
Much of the content of the press is intended solely for
its own day; and the journalist sometimes ruefully reflects that his art is one of improvisation, and that its
products, being destined to pass with the interest of
the moment, require no great care in their workmanship.
Yet, just because it is the day's report of itself, it is the
permanent word of that day to all other days. The press
must be free because its freedom is a condition of its
veracity; and its veracity is its good faith with the total
record of the human spirit.

At the same time, freedom of the press has to be
realized under two sets of limitations. The first is that
the several factors of an ideal press freedom are to some
extent incompatible with one another. The second is
that the free press is not an isolated value: it is a function within a society and must vary with the social context; it cannot mean the same in every society and at
all times. It is the remaining task of principle to indicate
what these varying conditions imply.

194

32. INCOMPATIBLE ELEMENTS OF IDEAL
PRESS FREEDOM

An ideally free press is free *from* compulsions from whatever source, governmental or social, external or internal: from compulsions—not, of course, from pressures, since no press can be free from pressures except in a moribund society empty of contending forces and beliefs. An ideally free press is free *for* the achievement of those goals of press service which its own instinct of workmanship and the requirements of the community combine to establish; and for these ends it must have command of all available technical resources, financial strength, reasonable access to sources of information at home and abroad, and the necessary staff and facilities for bringing its information and its judgments to the national market. An ideally free press would be free *to* all who have something worth saying to the public; and the selection of the voices thus deserving to be heard must be a free selection, arising from the preparatory processes of free speech, not from the desk of owner or editor alone.

To state these requirements of an ideal freedom is to indicate at once a pulling in opposite directions, from which some of the problems of the contemporary press arise. In fact, these several factors of an ideal press freedom are to some extent incompatible with one another. This will appear more explicitly if we bring together here some of the demands in behalf of freedom we have already made.

i. Full equipment always makes against free motion, like Saul's armor on David. A press which has grown to the measure of the national market and to the full use of technical resources can hardly be free from internal compulsions. The major part of the nation's press is large-scale enterprise, closely interlocked with the system of finance and industry; it will not without effort escape the natural bias of what it is. Yet this bias must be known and measurably overcome or counterbalanced if freedom is to remain secure.

ii. The ideal of the nation-wide press in a growing nation is increasingly difficult—through no one's fault—to combine with the ideal that every voice shall have the hearing it deserves. The extension of the major press toward national scope through consolidation or otherwise automatically renders less operative on a comparable scale the claims of potential issuers who have no press. For this clash there is no perfect remedy. There is relief through the multiplication of new instruments of manifolding and mass expression, and also through the effort of the wider press, somewhat as a common carrier, to assume responsibility for representing variant facets of opinion. But to represent all or any large number of such facets would only multiply confusion. No listening devices of the human mind have yet secured us from a certain wastage of human genius, as the scale of a nation's thinking enlarges. And the contemporary arts of what is called publicity—whose existence itself advertises the wide-felt need of special effort to secure recognition—cannot be acquitted, even at their best, of aiming rather at further lens distortion than at a just and proportionate publication of worth. As commercial arts, it is hard to see how justice can be their supreme object.

iii. The ancient antithesis between freedom and accountability remains as a practical problem. Accountabil-

ity, like subjection to law, is not necessarily a net subtraction from liberty; the affirmative factor of freedom,
freedom for, may be enhanced. But the liberty to be
carefree is gone. Charles Beard, earlier quoted (p. 12)
as saying that "in its origin, freedom of the press had
little or nothing to do with truth telling .... most of the
early newspapers were partisan sheets devoted to savage
attacks on party opponents," continues with the remark,
"Freedom of the press means the right to be just or
unjust, partisan or non-partisan, true or false, in news
column or editorial column."[1] Today, this former legal
privilege wears the aspect of social irresponsibility. The
press must know that its faults and errors have ceased
to be private vagaries and have become public dangers.
Its inadequacies menace the balance of public opinion.
It has lost the common and ancient human liberty to be
deficient in its function or to offer half-truth for the
whole.

The situation approaches a dilemma. The press must
remain private and free, *ergo*, human and fallible; but
the press dare no longer indulge in fallibility—it must
supply the public need. Here, again, there is no perfect
solution. But the important thing is that the press accept
the public standard and try for it. The legal right will
stand if the moral right is realized or tolerably approximated. There is a point beyond which failure to realize
the moral right will entail encroachment by the state
upon the existing legal right.

1. *St. Louis Post-Dispatch Symposium on Freedom of the Press,
1938*, p. 13.

33. THE VARIABLE MENTALITY OF THE CONSUMER

Conditions within the public itself set limits to what the press at any time can accomplish. The psychology of the consumer, including in his psychology the quality and force of his moral instincts, together with the social environment in which he moves and the press operates, are factors affecting the nature and scope of governmental responsibility as well as press achievement. They are variable factors which the press itself can influence.

The press is likely to forget that the public may not know what to demand of its press unless the press itself furnishes the instruction. Competition among press sources alone will hardly carry performance above what the public appears to want; and the self-discipline of the press will tend to be limited in its reach by the same set of facts. The realistic principle is that there is no use in supplying people with more or better than they want or can use; and that the best sign of what they require is what they are willing to pay for: "We can't be doing so badly, when you look at our circulation figures." There is a limited practical validity in this argument, but also an element of sophistry in the assumption that there is but one level at which demand and supply reach equilibrium; where all the competing services are at a low level, the consumer's choice can only be among several lows. He can hardly know, without seeing it, what it is that he misses; though he may realize that, of all marketable objects, truth is most defaced by being handled primarily as a commodity, with an eye in the main to the greatest appetites of the greatest number, and with a shrewd weather eye, in a few things, to the deft turn which protects one's greatest prejudice or promotes one's pet cause. With all the difficulty of resisting a *prima facie* lethargy of the public regarding quality,[2] it remains true that the level of demand is governed by the consumer's experience of what better can be had; the press *can educate demand*—this is one of its greatest functions and is, as we have pointed out, essentially inescapable.[3] The American press has frequently departed from strict business considerations to improve the quality of its work; with almost equal frequency it has found such departure eventually profitable. In any case, it belongs to the professional character of the press to take such risk; as Robert Redfield has put it, "We have to ask the press to be better than its public." Its positive service is always beyond the reach of any possible legal requirement, and it should receive credit where this is done. Where it is not done, we have to recognize the inherent difficulties of mass education, especially in times of social change. But we have also to consider the position of the consumer. To what extent is he helpless before what he is given, since it is only the press that can improve on

2. *The editor of* Harper's Magazine *has noted the difficulty of resisting pressure from readers or, as he says, "pressures from the editor's own zeal for more circulation than their standards of thoroughness or of honesty or of impartiality will permit without compromise. There are a great many readers—people who might become readers—who want the soothing, the specious, the innocuous, the easy. . . . . Sometimes the thought occurs to us that we are really idiots not to recognize that a magazine is just a commodity, and that we could probably sell more copies if we made everything short, easy, inoffensive, and trivial; or else that we just adopted a party line of some sort and made everything comfortable and profitably one-sided."*

3. See above, pp. 45–48.

the press? To what extent has he unrealized rights of the negative sort—rights not to be bamboozled, lied to, propagandized, monopolized by one type of editorial mind, even if it is a good type? What factors are affecting his power to shed the infections of press abuse and get at truth for himself? What are the factors affecting consumer's demand? Among them are:

a) *Variable immunity to lies and contamination.*—No man is wholly supine before press abuse. The grosser forms of fraud die out as the intelligence of the community increases; the results of a little detection are extraordinarily withering to the enthusiasm of the habitual liar. Given the rapidity with which an American community becomes wise to current trickery, deception has to be increasingly expert to be widely successful; the Barnum law holds good. But sophistication is a sad and retrospective wisdom; no immunity can keep pace with the progress of the arts of interested deceit, nor can any society protect its members in advance against them.

Nevertheless, a certain prophylaxis can be had. Not so much by early instruction in current motives and techniques of falsification. Immunity seems to be rather intuitive than analytic. It arises paradoxically from the shrewdness of a determined and practiced integrity. If our nation-wide customary education could include a stern training in the elementary scruples of thought and speech, that training would offer at once the best promise of a more scrupulous press and the best defense against unscruple.

b) *The liveliness of free authorities.*—No man's attitude to news report is made in a social vacuum. The press has seldom the deciding voice in making opinion. Each

consumer has his own authorities to which he freely
defers or with which he habitually compares his own
judgment—the personal authority of friends or groups
of friends (it would be worth inquiring how far public
opinion is made in clubs), the vague authority of custom,
the authority of the current image of success or happiness, the authority of science and of other professional
opinions including those of the clergy, the haunting in-
timations of perfection found in art or nature and which
guide the mind without the touch of any personal hand.
In proportion as these authorities are accessible and
active, and in proportion as their natural consensus is
realized, the judgments of the press encounter other
judgments; its information has to square accounts with
theirs. Steadying the reader's defense, they add an incentive to press reliability. And, in so far as they are active,
any relative local monopoly of press sources has a partial corrective; a liberating variety of aspects of opinion
can never be lacking.

Between the press and these other sources of opinion
guidance there tends to develop a certain division of
labor. By their nature, the novel and experimental aspects of any culture are "news." It would be an exaggeration to say that the press has a vested positional interest
in deviation, or a protective concern for the newborn
idea as for the newborn fact. But news emphasis is naturally on the as yet unknown and untried. And, while the
press in common with the rest of the community has its
standards of judgment, it is not its precise obligation to
distinguish between legitimate and meretricious experi-
mentation or between the scandal stirred by the work
of prophet or genius and the scandal which desires to

be mistaken for genius. The press is rather in the position of the witness who has to report what he observes, not to anticipate the outcome of the trial. This function of doorkeeper for innovation is of immense importance for a society unwilling to be wedded to fixity or to assume that the inherited social goals are the only ones. It is equally clear that the press emphasis alone is an element in abetting a psychology of change-for-change's sake; the health of society requires a continuous give-and-take between the press and other free sources of opinion.

c) The morale of the consumer.—The effectiveness of the self-righting tendencies within public discussion varies with the intelligence of the public, but it varies still more with the flux of temper and emotion.

Whether a person, or a public, faces a stream of press report with imagination to realize the bearing of what is said, with a mental energy and hope able to reduce a babel of tongues to a set of clear issues, or with a mud-pie lethargy into which impressions and ideas plump and sink, is a matter rather of feeling than of capacity. If there is anxiety in the background, or fear, or a suspiciousness for which every move of the object, person or nation appears ominous, or resentment toward an assumed source of injury, or a hating and punishing complex feeding on the secret penchant of the mind to have an ideal object of detestation, or envy—a hundred phases of the psychopathology of the consumer of news color the fringes of the text and alter the outcome of what we consider a process of public debate. Where minds are not only sturdy enough to be independent but also able to perceive their own biases and possessed both of the

202

good will and of the patience to be tolerant, the play of opinion in the market place will help them toward truth.

Where, on the other hand, the momentum of thought is feeble, and hunger is in the saddle, the demand of self-interest is likely to arbitrate issues of truth. Majority opinion is not pitched in disinterestedness at the scientific level. Where poverty presses on fear and pride, judgment of fact is lured to the side which promises bread and work. With economic distress the mass mind loses sight of its rational stars, and we face what is not normal to man, the economic determination of mass opinion.

If to economic need are added hatred and self-pity, the instruments of reflection are yielded to the control of the will to fight. It is never the whole of a public that is so seized; but, as long as there is a crowd element present capable of taking a theory as a guide for its sense of injury, there will be a wide-open opportunity for developing the more ominous public passions. It is here that men begin to doubt the sufficiency of freedom for the press. For when free citizens see demagogues at work, and the public authorities pledged to inaction by their own commitments to freedom, the temptation is strong to meet fire with fire and lie with lie. Much of the propaganda in the contemporary press is simply counter-propaganda, the work of well-meaning men who distort facts because they no longer know how to get a hearing for sober truth. The best press cannot insure that truth will be heard, as the negative passions insulate group from group.

Let the process go a stage further. Let the sense of injustice become ingrained, let history be read solely as furnishing fuel for resentment, then the common stock of human ideals is likely to be rejected as a set of blinds for the gullible, and the group mind may become the seat of a pestilence for which no opinion-forming process can yield a normal result. The free utterance of truth becomes futile.

This picture is not imaginary, though its original is in spots of pre-war Europe, not among ourselves. Some of its traits are here also. What we have to learn from it is that the justification of a free press is not absolute; it assumes a favorable temper of the mass-consumer's mind. This temper is open to various types of insidious decay. In our own society we are not a prey to the diseases of national futility or economic dread. Our psychopathology comes rather from the divisiveness incident to great energies uninformed by correspondingly firm common patterns of feeling and outlook; there is no uniting frame of symbol and belief within which readers read and thinkers think, of a texture adequate to the strains of our time. Without a fundamental emotional unity, a rain of facts and opinions through a press increasingly vehement in its own grooves has no tendency to build a public opinion. The press has tended to discount its own validity, and, as a result, the morale of its readers is low. They have been fed on too constant a diet of superlatives and excitements. They are fatigued by the incessant daily cries of new crises and new miseries, until they can no longer believe and respond to the real crisis and the real starvation. From public slogans and party platforms, shrill editorials and spiced-up news, to the insistent din and pretense of advertising, the reader or listener is attacked by the persistent deception of *excess*. He comes to believe that the careers of newsmen depend on the illicit transformation of narrative into melodrama; he refers all news materials to the limbo of half- and quarter-belief. He imagines propaganda both where it is and where it is not. And, in proportion as public credence is withdrawn from the press, the whole process of public thought, in the midst of unprecedented riches of news report and opinion, suffers from voluntary malnutrition.

The main evidence that the vigor of the public thought-process through the use of the press is below par is seen in the fact that government does take measures to supplement it. It acts, not directly on the press, but on the readers in their capacity as practically minded voters. It does not discontinue its appeal to their thought through party platform and press; but it does not rely on this type of persuasion for the fortunes of the party. The direct and indirect bribery, through patronage and preferment, which sustains our major party organizations is the tacit abandonment, by those who most loudly proclaim their faith in democracy, of the overt democratic process through the competition of opinion. When there is need to procure prompt public action, government has ways to elicit from Demos the response which, in its view, Demos ought to give; these ways do not invariably lead through the mind and conscience. In emergency the voices of the less responsible press may be gently secured through inducements irrelevant to the issues at stake, *ad majorem Dei gloriam*. The press remains free, but its functions are undermined.

34. THE NEARER SECURITIES OF PRESS FREEDOM

The press is capable of a more adequate self-regulation than it has hitherto exercised. It alone can hold itself to the positive standards of performance; it needs per- haps chiefly to have pointed out to it how fundamental its work is. Its major defects are within reach of a meas- ure of prompt correction. Incompetent reporting and comment on grave public issues cannot be wholly avoided, since reporters cannot be omniscient, and they must preserve, as Arthur Brisbane advised, their "super- ficiality"—their attachment to the current and visible phase of things. But they can be encouraged to use con- science, and they can achieve the grace of modesty and warn their readers that their version of truth is tentative. The photographers' outrageous violations of public meetings and personal privacy can be curbed without damage to their inestimable gift of the graphic record. A maturer responsibility can be taken for the educational possibilities of the qualitative aspects of the press, espe- cially those that have to do with the stabilities of social faith and the level of art and entertainment within the press including the cartoon. A readiness of the press to co-operate with private agencies and of private agencies to assume a greater measure of initiative in advising on press standards contain large promise of advance.

But within the community at large, also, there must be a profounder sense of responsibility for one's own thinking and for the level of emotional life, in recrea- tion and the use of leisure. The agencies of amusement and art touch the most potent springs of that emotional unity in which alone, through the meeting of minds, public discussion can be fruitful. This is why degradation of the arts through commercialized vulgarity, claiming the cover of freedom, stands out as so vital a blow to freedom. What men decide to enjoy is not purely a private concern. A vulgarized art elicits disintegrating rather than uniting emotions; and emotion is the energy of the will. If the agencies of amusement and art could recover a sense of the dignity of their social function, that of restoring vagrant feeling to a free acceptance of the good, the instinct of regulation—like an awkward gesture for recovering a lost balance—would be put to rest.

Unless in such ways as these the lifting element within our culture, which is by necessity spiritual and free, can find a route to its indispensable work, there is no certitude that a free press can or should remain wholly free.

APPENDIX

SUMMARY OF PRINCIPLE: A STATEMENT OF THE COMMISSION

Freedom of speech and press is close to the central meaning of all liberty. Where men cannot freely convey their thoughts to one another, no other liberty is secure. Where freedom of expression exists, the germ of a free society is already present and a means is at hand for every extension of liberty. Free expression is therefore unique among liberties as protector and promoter of the others; in evidence of this, when a regime moves toward autocracy, speech and press are among the first objects of restraint or control.

There are obvious reasons for bracketing freedom of the press with freedom of speech, as in the First Amendment. The press was at first hardly more than a means for extending the speaker's audience: the printed word could go far beyond the reach of his voice and to greater numbers and, through its durability, could continue to speak at all later time. This space-time extension alters nothing in the relation of the speaker to his audience or the nature of his message. And while today the voice, by the aid of radio, is freed from its natural limitations —it can reach as far as print, at least as many, and in far shorter time—it is the more evident that the two social functions merge.

Equally obvious are important differences between

speech and press. Speech is natural and inseparable from the human person, the breath of his social existence, and so intimate a tool of all mental life that without free speech thought itself could not be fully free. The press, by contrast, is an institution of developed society, a machine-using institution, and one whose role tends to enlarge as new instruments are devised. Extending many fold the working environment of personal life, it creates an appetite for its own increasing services. It has done much to make possible the unity of large states; without its aid the incipient order of mankind would be inconceivable. The problems it faces today are in large part the problems of its own achievements. It is incumbent upon us to inquire whether the traditional groundwork of principle which has inspired our existing law and our social attitudes is adequate to the period we now enter.

We shall begin by analyzing the situation of the press within society into its elements, in order to find the bare essentials of the actual fact we call "the press."

It will be understood that we are using the term "press" to include all means of communicating to the public news and opinions, emotions and beliefs, whether by newspapers, magazines, or books, by radio broadcasts, by television, or by films.

I. THE PARTIES DIRECTLY AT INTEREST

When we use the phrase "freedom of the press," we mention but one party at interest; the term "press" indicates an *issuer* of news, opinions, etc., through the media which reach mass audiences. But since no one cares to utter news or opinions into the void, there must be at least one other party at interest, the reader or listener as *consumer* of news, opinions, etc.; we shall refer to him collectively as the *audience*.

The interest of the issuer is, typically, to express his mind without external constraint or restraint—his ideas and reports of events, also his feelings, judgments, protests, business proposals, appeals, visions, prophecies. . . . . To the press, the implied audience is seldom visibly present or personally known; it is an imagined audience, and it is hopefully considered a representative audience. For, while it is commonly called "the public," it is at most a fair sample of the actual public. From this fragment, given freedom of speech, the message will spread to others and, with good luck, find the listeners to whom it belongs.

The interest of the consumer is, in detail, highly variable and personal. Yet, in any mentally alert society, there is a fairly universal desire for access to a world of experience, thought, and feeling beyond the range of private observation. And also beyond the range of private concern, for it is the genius of the human animal to "take an interest" in what does not immediately concern him. It may be a random and marginal curiosity; it may amount to an insistent hunger. In any case, since the nature of the appetite is such that it exceeds any actual satisfaction, the issuer can usually count on a latent demand; he may develop a demand where none pre-exists.

Wherever there are two parties, within a community, there is always a third party, the community itself. As a social totality including all pairs of (domestic) issuers and consumers, the community has a stake in the impact of all conversation, but especially in that of speech addressed to a mass audience. For all communication, apart from its direct meaning, has an effect on the communicators, on the social fabric, and on the common standards which measure the free cohesion of the group.

II. FREEDOM OF THE PARTIES AT INTEREST

Though the issuer's interest cannot be realized without an audience, his interest carries with it no claim whatever to compel the existence of an audience but only to invite an audience from men free not to listen. Freedom of the press must imply freedom of the consumer *not to consume* any particular press product; otherwise, the issuer's freedom could be at the expense of the consumer's freedom.

As the issuer cannot compel an audience, so the consumer cannot compel the existence of a speaker. Nor does it usually occur to him that he has a claim upon anyone for more light and leading than is spontaneously offered. The expresser is offering a gift. Nevertheless, the consumer is not a passive receptacle. Since the issuer cannot survive without his free attention, the consumer has power to encourage or discourage his advances. Through the consumer's willingness to pay for the successful divination of his appetites, he lures out the yield of thought-products; it is his free suffrage that builds up the great press and sustains a mass production in which thought and pseudo-thought devised for the market mix in varying proportions. He may go to the extent of setting up, with a like-minded group, a press organ to meet special group needs, interests, or prejudices; here the consumer controls, or perhaps becomes, the issuer. But the birth of opinion the consumer cannot control; the genesis of thought is incurably free and individual. For its abundance and pertinence he must take his chances as with the fertility of his native soil. He is necessarily interested in the freedom of the sources of opinion, because if they are unchecked and unwarped, even by himself, he will have, other things being equal, the widest and most honest offering to select from or to piece together or to mix with his own thought. His interest here coincides with that of the issuer, actual or potential.

Hence it is that, although there are these two direct interests, *only one of them, in simple conditions, needs protection.* To protect the freedom of the issuer is to protect the interest of the consumer and in general that of the community also. Hitherto in our history it has been sufficient to protect the "freedom of the press" as the freedom of issuers.

But, as this analysis is intended to indicate, under changed conditions the consumer's freedom might also require protection. If his need became more imperative, and if at the same time the variety of sources available to him were limited, as by concentration of the press industry, his freedom not to consume particular products of the existing press might vanish. It would then be no longer sufficient to protect the issuer alone. This theme is resumed in Section XI below. Meantime we trace the theory in terms of the issuer's freedom.

III. FREEDOM OF THE ISSUER REQUIRES PROTECTION

The utterance of opinion is not merely the announcement of an "I think. . . . ." It is a social force and is intended to be such.

Since civilized society is a working system of ideas, it lives and changes by the consumption of ideas. It is vulnerable to every shock to the fortunes of the ideas it embodies. And since there is usually less motive for uttering ideas with which everybody and every institution is in accord than for uttering those destined to change men's minds, a significant new idea in the social field is likely to arouse resistance. The issuer will have need of protection. But of what protection?

Freedom of expression can never be made a costless immunity by shackling hostile response, for response is also expression. Free expression is destined not to repress social conflict but to liberate it. But its intention is that the *level of social conflict shall be lifted from the plane of violence to the plane of discussion*. It should mean to the issuer that he is protected, not from anger, contempt, suffering, the loss of his clientele, for in this case his critic would be unfree, but from types of harm not an integral part of the argument or relevant to the argument (wrecking the issuer's shop, threatening his employees, intimidating his patrons. . . .).

There are those who would define freedom of expression as meaning no pain and no opprobrium to the issuer, no matter what he proposes. This ideal, if it is such, could be realized only in a society to which all ideas had become either impotent or indifferent. In any actual society free speech will require courage. And the first danger to free expression will always be the danger at the source, the timidity of the issuer, or his purchasability.

IV. THE EFFECTIVE AGENCIES FOR PROTECTING FREE EXPRESSION ARE THE COMMUNITY AND THE GOVERNMENT

The community acts, by routing social conflict through the ballot box, encouraging the method of discussion by making it a preliminary to action, and, then, by such traditions of self-restraint and toleration as may exist.

But, in the steadiest of communities, the struggle among ideas tends to become physical as it becomes prolonged; there is an incessant downtrend of debate toward the irrelevant exchange of punishments—malicious pressures, threats and bribes, broken windows and broken heads. Government is the only agency which, through its monopoly of physical force, can measurably insure that argument in speech and press will continue to be argument and not competitive injury. The elementary function of government in simply maintaining public order and the rights of person and property must be noted as the cornerstone of free expression, inasmuch as the cruder menaces to freedom are always from within the community.

Wherever in society there is an institution, a body of belief or interest, an organized power—good, bad, or mixed—there is a potential (we do not say actual) foe of the free critic—good, bad, or mixed. This potential hostility to the challenger is due not simply to the fact that it is easier and more natural for the obstinate vein in human nature to discourage or repress the critic than to meet his arguments. It is due also to irrational elements commonly present in the critic and the critic's audience. Freedom of the press to appeal to reason is liable to be taken as freedom to appeal to public passion, ignorance, prejudice, and mental inertia. We must not burke the fact that freedom of the press is dangerous. But there is no cure for bad argument either in refusing to argue or in substituting irrelevant pressures upon, or repression of, the free critic for the patient attempt to reach the elements of reasonableness in the mass mind, as long as the belief persists that such elements are there. The only hope for democracy lies in the validity of this belief and in the resolute maintenance, in that faith, of the critic's freedom.

The first line of defense for press freedom is government, as maintaining order and personal security and as exercising in behalf of press freedom the available sanctions against sabotage, blackmail, and corruption.

V. GOVERNMENT AS PROTECTING FREEDOM AGAINST GOVERNMENT

Any power capable of protecting freedom is also capable of infringing freedom. This is true both of the community and of government. In modern society the policy of government vis-à-vis the free expression of its citizens is in peculiar need of definition.

For every modern government, liberal or otherwise, has a specific position in the field of ideas; its stability is vulnerable to critics in proportion to their ability and persuasiveness. To this rule, a government resting on

popular suffrage is no exception. On the contrary, just
to the extent that public opinion is a factor in the tenure
and livelihood of officials and parties, such a government
has its own peculiar form of temptation to manage the
ideas and images entering public debate.

If, then, freedom of the press is to achieve reality,
government must set limits upon its capacity to interfere with, regulate, control, or suppress the voices of
the press or to manipulate the data on which public
judgment is formed.

What we mean by a free society is chiefly one in which
government does thus expressly limit its scope of action
in respect to certain human liberties, namely, those liberties which belong to the normal development of mature
men. Here belong free thought, free conscience, free
worship, free speech, freedom of the person, free assembly. Freedom of the press takes its place with these.
And all of them, together with some stipulations regarding property, constitute the burden of our bills of rights.

VI. FREE EXPRESSION AS A RIGHT

If government accepts a limitation of its range of
action in view of such interests, the reason is that they
are not only important interests but also moral rights.
And they are moral rights because their exercise, besides
being valuable to both the citizen and the community,
has an aspect of duty about it.

The motives of expression are certainly not all dutiful;
they are and should be as multiform as human emotion
itself, grave and gay, casual and purposeful, artful and
idle. In a modern state all social activity, including the

conduct of business, requires use of the press as well as of speech and assumes its natural freedom. But there is a vein of expression which has the added impulsion of duty, namely, the expression of thought and belief. If a man is burdened with an idea, he not only desires to express it, he ought to express it. The socially indispensable functions of criticism and appeal may be as abhorrent to the diffident as they are attractive to the pugnacious, but for neither is the issue one of wish. It is one of obligation—to the community and also to something beyond the community, let us say, to truth.[1] It is the duty of the scientist to his result and of Socrates to his oracle; but it is equally the duty of every man to his own belief. Because of this duty to what is beyond the state, freedom of speech and press are moral rights which the state must not infringe.

While dutiful utterance bears the burden of the claim of right as against the state, that right extends its coverage over all legitimate expression.

This self-limitation of the state cannot in the long run be contrary to the public interest. For, whatever its judgment of the opinions expressed, no nation can have a net interest in repressing the conscience of its citizens. On the contrary, the modern state recognizes that the

1. *For brevity, we shall use the concern for "truth" as token of a group of interests having a similar claim on expression, such as belief regarding "right," or justice of feeling, or public policy, or the advocacy of a legitimate personal interest. To make "truth" the symbol of all this will bring our discussion into close relation with the classical argument for freedom of expression, which has been chiefly concerned with the contest of opinions in respect to truth and falsehood. "Truth" is beyond the state and may symbolize whatever is, in similar fashion, obligatory on individual and state alike.*

citizen's conscience is a source of its own continued vitality. And, wherever the citizen has a duty of conscience, there the sovereign state has also a duty, namely, to that conscience of its citizen. Thus both its interest and its duty require the state to give the moral right a legal status.

This consideration is logically prior to the traditional ground of a free press, namely, that the unhampered publication of opinion promotes the "victory of truth over falsehood" in the public arena. Public discussion is indeed a necessary condition of a free society, and freedom of expression is a necessary condition of an amply furnished public discussion. It is not a sufficient condition, for the co-presence of a variety of opinions is not equivalent to debate; it may well be questioned whether the actual process we now call public discussion is functioning as the health of a democracy requires. In any case, it is a process which elicits mental power and breadth in those consumers whom it does not baffle or confuse; it is essential to building a mentally robust public; and, without something of the kind, no self-governing society could operate. But the original source of supply for this very process is the duty of the individual thinker to his thought; here is the primary ground of his right.

While it is not, like the right of speech, a universal right that every citizen should own a press or be an editor or have access to the clientele of any existing press, it is the whole point of a free press that ideas deserving a public hearing shall get a public hearing and that the decision of what ideas deserve that hearing shall rest in part with the public, not solely with the particular biases of editors and owners. In any populous community a vigorous trimming-out process among ideas presenting themselves for wide public hearing is obviously essential; but freedom of the press becomes a mockery unless this selective process is free also. This means that free speech, with its informal emphases, is the natural vestibule to a free press and that the circumstance of ownership of press instruments confers no privilege of deafness toward ideas which the normal selective processes of the community promote to general attention.[2]

VII. THE MORAL RIGHT OF FREEDOM OF EXPRESSION IS NOT UNCONDITIONAL

If reasons can be given for a claim of right—and there are reasons for all of them—those reasons constitute the condition on which the right can be claimed. The absence of that condition, therefore, automatically removes the basis for the claim.

By this logic, since the claim of the right of free expression is based on the duty of a man to his thought, then when this duty is ignored or rejected—as when the issuer is a liar, an editorial prostitute whose political judgments can be bought, a malicious inflamer of unjust hatred—the ground for his claim of right is nonexistent. In the absence of accepted moral duties there are no moral rights.

2. *It is worth noting that the Soviet Constitution, while limiting publishable ideas within a fixed orthodoxy, undertakes within these limits to implement press expression for a wide segment of the people who own no presses. It provides (Art. 125) that "printing presses, stocks of paper . . . . communications facilities, and other material requisites" shall be put at the disposal of working people and their organizations.*

It may reasonably be doubted whether any man is capable of a thoroughgoing repudiation of duty. His experiments in the rejection of good faith are likely to be sporadic; a single lie does not make a man a liar nor a single acceptance of bribe a prostitute. Further, if a man is stung into reckless or inflammatory speech by a genuine grievance which ought to be made known, his bedeviled utterance may contain an important piece of truth. Still, if we define a liar as a man who habitually tells the truth except when it suits his policy to deviate, the press liar is not a mythical person. His ultimate humanity and freedom he cannot alienate; but he has used his freedom to undermine his freedom. His claim of right as an issuer of opinion has by his own choice become groundless.

Since all rights, moral or legal, make assumptions regarding the will of the claimants, there are no unconditional rights. The notion of rights, costless, unconditional, conferred by the Creator at birth, was a marvelous fighting principle against arbitrary governments and had its historical work to do. But in the context of an achieved political freedom the need of limitation becomes evident. The unworkable and invalid conception of birthrights, wholly divorced from the condition of duty, has tended to beget an arrogant type of individualism which makes a mockery of every free institution, including the press. This conception has concealed the sound basis of our liberal polity, the one natural right, the right to do one's human task. From this one right, the others can be derived so far as they are valid; and into this right the ingredient of duty is inseparably built.

VIII. A RIGHT OF LIBERTY INCLUDES A RIGHT TO BE IN ERROR

Liberty is experimental, and experiment implies trial and error. Debate itself could not exist unless wrong opinions could be rightfully offered by those who suppose them to be right. For social purposes, the cutting edge of the right of free expression is its demand for what is called "toleration" on the part of those who see, or think they see, error in others. What is required is something more positive than toleration—respect for the process of self-correction as against any authoritatively imposed correctness.

The assumption of this respect is that the man in error is actually trying for the truth; and this effort on his part is of the essence of his claim to freedom. What the moral right does not cover is a right to be deliberately or irresponsibly in error.

IX. THE ABUSE OF A RIGHT DOES NOT IPSO FACTO FORFEIT THE PROTECTION OF THE LEGAL RIGHT

Legal protection cannot vary with the inner fluctuations of moral direction in individual wills; it does not cease whenever the moral ground of right has been personally abandoned. It is not even desirable that the whole area of the responsible use of freedom should be made legally compulsory, even if such a thing were possible, for in that case free self-control, necessary ingredient of any free state, would be superseded by mechanism.

The attempt to correct abuses of freedom, including press freedom, by resort to legal penalties and controls is the first spontaneous impulse of reform. But the dangers of the cure must be weighed against the dangers of the disease; every definition of an abuse invites abuse of the definition. The law might well be justified in acting against malicious public criticism; but if courts were called on to determine the inner corruptions of intention, honest and necessary criticism would proceed under an added peril and the "courage of disclosure" incur a new cost.

Hence many a lying, venal, and scoundrelly public expression must continue to find shelter under a "freedom of the press" built for widely different ends. There is a practical presumption against the use of legal action to curb press abuse.

X. THERE ARE, HOWEVER, LIMITS TO THE LEGAL TOLERATION OF ABUSE OF THE LIBERTY OF EXPRESSION

The already recognized areas of legal correction of misused liberty in this field—libel, misbranding, obscenity, incitement to riot, sedition in case of clear and present danger—have a common principle, namely, that an utterance or publication invades in a serious, overt, and demonstrable manner recognized private rights or vital social interests. If new categories of abuse come within this definition, the extension of legal remedies is justified. In view of the general presumption against legal action above stated, the burden of proof will rest upon those who would extend these categories; but the presumption is not intended to render society supine in the face of all new types of misuse, actual or possible, of the immense powers of the contemporary press.

Today a further question of public responsibility in the use of freedom is raised in view of the extent to which the function of the press is affected by a public interest. Not only positive misdeeds but omissions and inadequacies of press performance have now a bearing on general welfare. Freedom to express has hitherto included freedom to refrain from expressing; for the press this liberty is no longer perfect.

XI. THE WORK OF THE PRESS AS CLOTHED WITH A PUBLIC INTEREST

As observed at the beginning (Sec. I), the work of the press always involves the interest of the consumer; but, as long as the consumer is free, his interest is protected in the protection of the freedom of the issuer. Today, however, the conditions affecting the consumer's freedom have radically altered. Through concentration of ownership the flow of news and opinion is shaped at the sources; its variety is limited; and at the same time the insistence of the consumer's need has increased. He is dependent on the quality, proportion, and extent of his news supply not alone for his personal access to the world of thought and feeling but also for the materials of his business as a citizen in judging public affairs. With this situation any community in which public opinon is a factor in policy, domestic and international, must be deeply concerned.

Clearly a qualitatively new era of public responsibility for the press has arrived; and it becomes an imperative question whether press performance can any longer be left to the unregulated initiative of the issuers. The moral and legal right of thinkers to utter their opinions must in any case remain intact; this right stands for the kernel of individualism at the heart of all free social life. But the element of duty involved in the right requires a new scrutiny. And the service of news, as distinct from the utterance of opinion, acquires an added importance. The need of the consumer to have adequate and uncontaminated mental food is such that he is under a duty to get it; and, because of this duty, his interest acquires the stature of a *right*. It becomes legitimate to speak of the moral right of men to the news they can use.

Since the consumer is no longer free not to consume, and can get what he requires only through existing press organs, protection of the freedom of the issuer is no longer sufficient to protect automatically either the consumer or the community. The general policy of laissez faire in this field must be reconsidered.

XII. THE ACCOUNTABLE PRESS AND THE RESPONSIBLE COMMUNITY

The press today, as the Supreme Court has recently recognized in the case of news services, has responsibilities to the general spread of information which present analogies to those of a common carrier or of a trustee, though the likeness in either of these cases is limited. The analogy is closer to an educational enterprise in which private schools, enjoying the advantages and risks of experimental initiative, are yet performing a necessary public function for which a measure of social accountability would be appropriate. Do these analogies suggest that for the press also some degree of public oversight and co-operation and possibly of regulation must be the way of the future?

An over-all social responsibility for the quality of press service to the citizen cannot be escaped; the community cannot wholly delegate to any other agency the ultimate responsibility for a function in which its own existence as a free society may be at stake.

At the same time, the main positive energy for the improvement of press achievement must come from the issuers. Although the standards of press performance arise as much from the public situation and need as from the conscious goals of the press, these standards must be administered by the press itself. This means that *the press must now take on the community's press objectives as its own objectives*. And for the correction of abuses the maxim holds good that self-correction is better than outside correction, so long as self-correction holds out a reasonable and realistic hope, as distinct from lip service to piously framed paper codes.

How shall this realism be implemented? And how shall the objectives of the press he held to identity with the necessary objectives of the community? By a recognition on the part of the press that, while its enterprise is and should remain a private business, its efforts to define and realize its standards are also a community concern and should be systematically associated with corresponding efforts of community, consumers, and government.

—With those of consumers and community, acting through specialized organs, as responsible critic, gadfly, and source of incentive.

—With those of government in various ways whose principles we may indicate as follows:

1. Without intruding on press activities, government may act to improve the conditions under which they take place so that the public interest is better served— as by making distribution more universal and equable, removing hindrances to the free flow of ideas, reducing confusion and promoting the reality of public debate.

2. New legal remedies and preventions are not to be excluded as aids to checking the more patent abuses of the press, under the precautions we have emphasized. Such legal measures are not in their nature subtractions from freedom but, like laws which help to clear the highways of drunken drivers, are means of increasing freedom, through removing impediments to the practice and repute of the honest press.

3. Government may and should enter the field of press comment and news supply, not as displacing private enterprise, but as a supplementary source. In so doing, it may present standards for private emulation. While in our experience a democratic government is one in which government itself is one of the main objects of public discussion and can therefore never be allowed to control or to regulate the debate, it is not inconceivable that a government by the people should also be a powerful instrument for the people, in respect to educational and other noncommercial possibilities of the developing press.

XIII. RESULTING CONCEPTION OF FREEDOM
OF THE PRESS

The emerging conception of freedom of the press may be summarized as follows:

As with all freedom, press freedom means freedom from and also freedom for.

A free press is free from compulsions from whatever source, governmental or social, external or internal. From compulsions, not from pressures; for no press can be free from pressures except in a moribund society empty of contending forces and beliefs. These pressures, however, if they are persistent and distorting—as financial, clerical, popular, institutional pressures may become—approach compulsions; and something is then lost from effective freedom which the press and its public must unite to restore.

A free press is free for the expression of opinion in all its phases. It is free for the achievement of those goals of press service on which its own ideals and the requirements of the community combine and which existing techniques make possible. For these ends it must have full command of technical resources, financial strength, reasonable access to sources of information at home and abroad, and the necessary facilities for bringing information to the national market. The press must grow to the measure of this market.

For the press there is a third aspect of freedom. The free press must be free to all who have something worth saying to the public, since the essential object for which a free press is valued is that ideas deserving a public hearing shall have a public hearing.

XIV. CONTEMPORARY PROBLEMS OF PRINCIPLE

1. These several factors of an ideal press freedom are to some extent incompatible with one another.

A press which has grown to the measure of the national market and to the full use of technical resources can hardly be free from internal compulsions. The major part of the nation's press is large-scale enterprise, closely interlocked with the system of finance and industry; it will not without effort escape the natural bias of what it is. Yet, if freedom is to remain secure, this bias must be known and overcome.

Again, the growth of the press acts together with the growth of the nation to make more remote the ideal that every voice shall have the hearing it deserves. Concentration of power substitutes one controlling policy for many independent policies, lessens the number of major competitors, and renders less operative the claims of potential issuers who have no press. For this clash there is no perfect remedy. There is relief, to the extent that the wider press, somewhat as a common carrier, assumes responsibility for representing variant facets of opinion. But no listening devices of the human mind have yet secured us from a certain wastage of human genius as the scale of a nation's thinking enlarges; and the contemporary arts of what is called publicity can hardly be acquitted of aiming rather at further lens distortion than at just and proportionate recognition of worth. As commercial arts it is hard to see how they can make justice their supreme object.

2. There is an antithesis between the current conception of the freedom of the press and the accountability of the press.

Accountability, like subjection to law, is not necessarily a net subtraction from liberty; the affirmative factor of freedom, freedom for, may be enhanced. But the liberty to be carefree is gone. Charles Beard could say with accuracy that "in its origin, freedom of the press had little or nothing to do with truth telling . . . . most of the early newspapers were partisan sheets devoted to savage attacks on party opponents. . . . . Freedom of the press means the right to be just or unjust, partisan or non-partisan, true or false, in news column or editorial column."[3] Today, this former legal privilege wears the aspect of social irresponsibility. The press must know that its faults and errors have ceased to be private vagaries and have become public dangers. Its inadequacies menace the balance of public opinion. It has lost the common and ancient human liberty to be deficient in its function or to offer half-truth for the whole.

The situation approaches a dilemma. The press must remain private and free, *ergo* human and fallible; but the press dare no longer indulge in fallibility—it must supply the public need. Here, again, there is no perfect solution. But the important thing is that the press accept the public standard and try for it. The legal right will stand if the moral right is realized or tolerably approximated. There is a point beyond which failure to realize the moral right will entail encroachment by the state upon the existing legal right.

3. *St. Louis Post-Dispatch Symposium on Freedom of the Press, 1938*, p. 13.

XV. THE ENDURING GOAL AND THE
VARIABLE REALIZATION

A free press is not a passing goal of human society; it is a necessary goal. For the press, taken in sum, is the swift self-expression of the experience of each moment of history; and this expression ought to be true. Much of the content of the press is intended solely for its own day; and the journalist sometimes reflects that his art is one of improvisation, and that its products, being destined to pass with the interest of the moment, require no great care in their workmanship. Yet, just because it is the day's report of itself, it is the permanent word of that day to all other days. The press must be free because its freedom is a condition of its veracity, and its veracity is its good faith with the total record of the human spirit.

At the same time, freedom of the press is certainly not an isolated value, nor can it mean the same in every society and at all times. It is a function within a society and must vary with the social context. It will be different in times of general security and in times of crisis; it will be different under varying states of public emotion and belief.

The freedom we have been examining has assumed a type of public mentality which may seem to us standard and universal, but which is, in many respects, a product of our special history—a mentality accustomed to the noise and confusion of clashing opinions and reasonably stable in temper when the fortunes of ideas are swiftly altered. But what a mind does with a fact or an opinion is widely different when that mind is serene and when it is anxious; when it has confidence in its environment and when it is infected with suspicion or resentment; when it is gullible and when it is well furnished with the means of criticism; when it has hope and when it is in despair.

Further, the consumer is a different man when he has to judge his press alone and when his judgment is steadied by other social agencies. Free and diverse utterance may result in bewilderment unless he has access—through home, church, school, custom—to interpreting patterns of thought and feeling. There is no such thing as press "objectivity" unless the mind of the reader can identify the objects dealt with.

Whether at any time and place the psychological conditions exist under which a free press has social significance is always a question of fact, not of theory. These mental conditions may be lost. They may also be created. The press itself is always one of the chief agents in destroying or in building the bases of its own significance.

ROBERT M. HUTCHINS   ARCHIBALD MacLEISH

ZECHARIAH CHAFEE, JR.   CHARLES E. MERRIAM

JOHN M. CLARK   REINHOLD NIEBUHR

JOHN DICKINSON   ROBERT REDFIELD

WILLIAM E. HOCKING   BEARDSLEY RUML

HAROLD D. LASSWELL   ARTHUR M. SCHLESINGER

GEORGE N. SHUSTER

INDEX

PUBLICATIONS OF THE COMMISSION

A Free and Responsible Press: A General Report on Mass Communication: Newspapers, Radio, Motion Pictures, Magazines, and Books. By the COMMISSION ON FREEDOM OF THE PRESS. With a Foreword by ROBERT M. HUTCHINS. Chicago, 1947.

This report presents the general analysis and conclusions of the Commission with regard to the principles, problems, performance, and defects of the press in the United States today—defining the press broadly to include newspapers, radio, motion pictures, magazines, and books. The influences leading to concentration of ownership, the centralization of news sources, action of pressure groups, and government regulation of the flow of information in relation to freedom are reviewed. The requirements for current information which modern society by necessity imposes on the agencies of mass communication are defined. Suggestions and recommendations designed to promote responsible or accountable freedom of the press are made.

In addition to the *General Report* and the present study by Mr. Hocking, the following special studies under the authorship of individual members of the Commission or its staff have been published or are being prepared for publication:

1. *Government and Mass Communications.* By ZECHARIAH CHAFEE, JR., professor of law, Harvard University. Chicago, 1947.

An extensive analysis of the threefold relation of government to mass communication: (1) the use of governmental power to limit or to suppress discussion, (2) affirmative governmental action to encourage better and more extensive communication, and (3) government as a party to communication.

The two volumes cover the whole field of governmental and legal regulation of the press under peacetime conditions, with special attention to certain areas where proposals are currently made to alter existing statutory, judicial, or administrative practice. These include libel and compulsory correction of published errors, postoffice mail-exclusion orders and denial of second-class privileges, compulsory disclosure of source, laws requiring collective bargaining, and antitrust statutes as applied to the press industries. The author's recommendation regarding many of these problems is included.

2. *Peoples Speaking to Peoples.* By LLEWELLYN WHITE, assistant director, and ROBERT D. LEIGH, director of the Commission on Freedom of the Press. Chicago, 1946.

An extensive analysis of international mass communication, based upon a threefold Commission program of (1) improving physical transmission facilities, (2) lessening political and economic restrictions on the free flow of words and images across borders, and (3) improving the accuracy, representative character, and quality of the words and images transmitted. The authors review the development of the physical instruments and processes in international communication, including the newer facilities of voice, dot-dash and facsimile broadcast radio transmission, the organization of press associations, and books and periodicals in the international field. They analyze proposals for merger of telecommunication facilities, for multilateral and bilateral treaties designed to reduce barriers and to promote freer access to information, for export federations in books and the voice-boadcasting fields, and for international agencies to regulate physical transmission, to lessen political and economic restrictions on information, and to inquire into violations of free-press treaties. They make specific recommendations in relation to each of these matters and propose a related government-industry program to guarantee that the whole field of communication between peoples will be adequately covered.

3. *Freedom of the Movies.* By RUTH A. INGLIS, research staff, Commission on Freedom of the Press, assistant professor of sociology, University of Washington. Chicago, 1947.

Freedom of the Movies is a study of self-regulation, Hollywood's own means of controlling the content of films as they are produced. The purpose of self-regulation is to prevent cuts and rejections by the half-dozen state and many municipal censor boards and to avoid trouble with moralistic and other pressure groups. The principles and rules of the Production Code and its administration by the Johnston Office (long the Hays Office) are described fully in the book so that the reader may ponder them for himself.

Having studied self-regulation in the light of the growing criticism of the movies on the ground that they are silly, insignificant, and lacking in artistic integrity, the author offers concrete suggestions for achieving a vital screen which at the same time is not obscene or indecent. The author's specific proposals for the improvement of self-regulation will command the attention of those who have felt that the movies have been too sensitive to certain segments of the community and unmindful of certain nonreligious social values.

4. *The American Radio.* By LLEWELLYN WHITE, assistant director of the Commission on Freedom of the Press. Chicago, 1947.

A story of radio's first quarter-century—its amazing physical growth, its economic and artistic development, its attempt at self-regulation, the government's attempt to regulate it, and the consumer's attitude toward it. The author applies to the broadcasting industry the yardstick of accountability for performing an important intelligence function, defines the points of defect, and makes definite proposals for improvement which take account of the technological developments now on the way or on the horizon.

5. *The American Press and the San Francisco Conference.* By MILTON D. STEWART. With an Introduction by HAROLD D. LASSWELL, of the Yale University Law School.

A systematic study, on a comparative basis, of the treatment given the San Francisco Conference by the general newspaper and periodical press, press associations, radio, films, and special-group publications. The need for a positive as well as a negative conception of freedom is discussed, and standards are proposed as an essential tool for gauging the freedom and the accountability of the press in actual operation. This is followed by statistical summaries and examples of the levels of performance reached in covering the first United Nations conference by about seventy daily newspapers, forty general magazines, the four major radio networks, the five leading newsreels, and several hundred group publications. Comparisons of achievement within each medium and among the media are made.